# THE · FILMS · OF
# ROBERT · ALTMAN

## BY · ALAN · KARP

THE SCARECROW PRESS, INC.
METUCHEN, N.J., & LONDON
1   9   8   1

**Library of Congress Cataloging in Publication Data**

Karp, Alan, 1947-
    The films of Robert Altman.

    Bibliography: p.
    Includes index.
    1. Altman, Robert, 1925-    . I. Title.
PN1998.A3A5765    791.43'023'0924 [B]  80-29501
ISBN 0-8108-1408-0

For Jean

# PREFACE

The films of Robert Altman have been praised to the hilt and damned with a passion. Pauline Kael has called NASHVILLE "the funniest epic vision of America ever to reach the screen," while words like "pretentious" and "indulgent" have become commonplace in the vocabulary of his detractors. This book attempts to enlighten the uninitiated and stimulate the devotees, by providing them with a thorough roadmap to the inadequately explored environs of Altmanville. Along the way, a great deal of discussion is devoted to such Altman trademarks as the use of overlapping dialogue, elliptical narratives, and the moving camera, although by journey's end it should be clear that there are many other reasons for placing Altman at the cutting edge of American film culture.

I would like to take this opportunity to thank John Fell, Howard Suber, Carl Mueller, Jack Kolb, Michael Jones, and Stephen Mamber, in particular, for their comments on my manuscript. I also wish to acknowledge Richard Thompson's helpful suggestions and the use of his research materials. And, finally, Jan Kerwin and Ana Blanco's help in the actual preparation of the manuscript deserves to be duly noted.

Alan Karp
Los Angeles
September 1980

# TABLE OF CONTENTS

CHAPTER I

INTRODUCTION: THE FILMS OF ROBERT ALTMAN

While defending one of his motion pictures (Luna), the
Italian director Bernardo Bertolucci made several statements
that are particularly relevant to the present study.  Exemplifying a distinctly European point of view, Bertolucci complained
that the American critics' reliance on their own subjective
opinions was an irresponsible substitute for analysis.  Instead
of merely flaunting their own egos, Bertolucci insisted that
these critics should first try to understand what they are looking at, and second, that they should help their readers to understand "movies that are different."  Essentially, Bertolucci's
admonition has provided me with a remarkably succinct summary of what I have tried to do with the films of Robert Altman.  Because, quite simply, Altman's movies are "different."
What I am most concerned with is the "how" and the "why."
How are they different, and why should we care?

At the same time, it is hoped not only that this study
will illuminate Altman's work per se, but that it will also
shed light on general issues that arise out of the modernist
context in which Altman works.  The first step in such a
process necessarily involves the establishment of a series of
definitions, which must then be integrated into analyses of the
films themselves.  For example, what is this "modernist context," and how is it relevant to the present undertaking?  My
own view is that this is an extremely important starting point,
as the way in which modernism is variously defined is at the
root of a great deal of needless controversy.  Consequently,
this introduction has been designed to put this question and
other related biographical material into the kind of historical
perspective that will enable us to gain a clearer understanding
of Altman's cinematic achievements.

As described by Susan Sontag in On Photography, the
concept of modernism has become a contradiction in terms.
Her reasoning goes something like this:  contemporary aud-

1

iences are less and less willing to be serious "in that old-
fashioned way that modernist art demands." However, as
she goes on to say, there is also a side of modernism that
embraces the idea of antiart (i. e. , pop art, minimalism, and
"the Warhol aesthetic"). It is in this sense that Sontag characterizes modernism itself as both a breeding ground for works
of contemporary art and as a concept that contained the seeds
of its own destruction.

What happened was that "too much emphasis was placed
on outrage, and people got used to taking short cuts. Enough
artists said we had to close the gap between art and life.
Now people aren't willing to put in the work involved in entering these realms of discourse which distinguish art from life."
Thus, "when modernism became the established mode, it also
became a contradiction in terms."[1] But, we must now ask,
how valid are Sontag's assumptions, and do they really apply
to film? The answer, I think, is both yes and no. That is,
modernism does not seem to have come even close to becoming the established mode in film, unless it is equated with Sontag's overdetermined notion of it. My point is that the idea
of modernism in film is all but inseparable from the concept
of subjective sectors of reality. In other words, Sontag herself has said that she came to realize that she wasn't really
writing about photography so much as she was writing about
modernity and "the way we look at the world today." Who is
looking at the world? We look. But who is doing the writing? Susan Sontag.

Another way to illustrate this point would be to consider
the fact that because many of the most widely discussed films
of the past ten or fifteen years that have been described as
"modernist" (Last Year at Marienbad, Persona, Performance,
Wind from the East, etc. ) make considerable demands upon
the viewer, they are usually referred to as "difficult" films.
But "difficulty" is a relative factor, which is equally dependent upon the viewer's disposition, intelligence, capacity for
interpretation, and the structural organization of the film or
text. The failure to acknowledge this basic condition of spectator interaction is the cause of many fruitless critical dis-
putes.

More often than not, the dual nature of film as both
a business and art results in films that reinforce audience
suspicions and expectations. Thus, as audiences became ac-
customed to the "modernist" techniques used by many New
Wave filmmakers in the 1960s, these techniques were reab-

sorbed into the commercial mainstream in films like The Wild
Bunch (i. e. , in the slow-motion "bloodbath ballet"), Butch
Cassidy and the Sundance Kid (the freeze-frame ending), Play
It Again, Sam (intensified self-reference gravitating toward
self-parody), and Network, a film that has turned a devas-
tating attack on its closest competitor into a very profitable
business venture.  More recently, mass audiences have been
exposed to the exquisite irony of seeing a heavily edited version of Network on the tube.  TV movies are glutted with further examples of ways in which what were once considered to
be innovative techniques have been transformed into tired formulas.  The upshot of all this is that the increased use of various techniques and the style in which they are employed has
served to change prevailing cinematic codes, the way we look
at films, and film criticism itself.

As implied at the outset, this introduction can do little
more than touch upon some of the more hotly contested issues
in contemporary film criticism as a prelude to an examination
of Altman's work.  In so doing, I have found it useful to at
least allude to some of those New Wave films that are largely
responsible for sparking the modernist debate, because Altman
owes a much larger debt to this European tradition than he
does to that of his native land.  In fact, Altman's European
leanings, together with his apparent inability to feel himself
to be a part of any existing American tradition of filmmaking,
has been one of the most influential factors on his career.
These "leanings" can be conveniently summarized under three
major headings.  In brief, the first of these has to do with
the concept of a director as the prime mover of the work--
as the person who puts a personal stamp on the film no matter how varied the original material might be.  The second
heading involves the idea of the director as a "serious artist,"
who, in Altman's own words, is "an enemy of the multitude."

Now, because such phrases as "serious artist" are so
obviously overdetermined (i. e. , open to infinite interpretations),
I have decided to borrow Arthur Koestler's neologism "bisociation" in an effort to define my meaning more accurately.
In The Act of Creation, Koestler uses this term "to make a
distinction between the routine skills of thinking on a single
'plane,' and the creative act," which (Koestler argues) always
operates on more than one plane.  Moreover, this process of
bisociation is seen to be central to both the creation of art-
works and to their consumption.  Accordingly, most "serious"
films and novels are seen to contain an element of the riddle
that the spectator must solve through a process of imaginative

recreation.  In this way, Koestler contrasts the serious work
of art to "the type of entertainment dished out by the mass
media [which] makes one apt to forget that true recreation is
re-creation."[2]  Undoubtedly, this is at best a rather superficial account of Koestler's argument, which will be ampli-
fied shortly.  But for the time being, suffice it to say that
most of Altman's work embraces this notion of seriousness
and in so doing runs counter to the bulk of American (as opposed to European) feature films.  To put it another way,
Altman is at odds with our industry's fear that serious filmmaking in the European mold is somehow inimical to the
American cinema's traditionally based function as the purvey-
or of a more "pure" entertainment experience.  In saying
this, however, I must caution the reader that my statements
are not meant to denigrate this tradition, but merely to make
certain distinctions that are necessary to a more thorough
understanding of Altman's approach to filmmaking.  Such an
approach differs greatly from that epitomized by another famous American director, who once said, "My name is John
Ford and I make westerns."

     The third area of confluence between Altman and his
European counterparts has to do with affinities of form and
style.  If we return for a moment to Arthur Koestler's work,
his use of the terms "emphasis" and "implication" could
prove quite revealing in the present context.  Very briefly,
"emphasis is a means of suggestion."  It creates "suspense
and facilitates the listener's flow of association along habit-
formed channels."  Koestler states that in more sophisticated
forms of art, suggestion through emphasis is not enough ("it
can defeat its own purpose").  Accordingly, "it must be compensated by the opposite kind of virtue:  the exercise of 'economy,' or, more precisely, the technique of 'implication.'"
"Implication," then, serves to shift the burden of the riddle
to the reader.  It creates "logical gaps which the [reader]
has to bridge by his own effort:  he is forced to cooperate."

     Koestler calls the logical bridging of gaps by filling
in the missing links "interpolation."  A related type of operation is "transformation," or "reinterpretation of the given
data into some analogous terms."  Both of these operations
are seen to comprise the transformation of metaphorical into
literal statements.  Applying these concepts to Altman's
oeuvre, we can see the complementary techniques of emphasis and implication as virtual metaphors for the process of
filmmaking that several theorists have referred to as the
"open text."

> In fact, both techniques have their roots in the bas-
> ic mechanism of communicating thoughts by word
> or sign.   Language itself is never completely ex-
> plicit.   Words have suggestive, evocative powers;
> but at the same time they are merely stepping
> stones for thought.   Economy means spacing them
> at intervals just wide enough to require a signifi-
> cant effort from the receiver of the message; the
> artist rules his subjects by turning them into ac-
> complices. [3]

This explanation also goes a long way toward elaborating
what Altman meant when he said that his aim "is to meet
the audience halfway."   Similarly, it provides us with an alternative description of the narrative strategies employed by
many of the New Wave directors.

Taking this line of thought one step further, Altman's
films, like those of the best New Wave directors, can most
profitably be viewed as both a representation of, and a reaction against, their cultural milieu.   Moreover, Altman's
opposition to what might be termed the "other-directed"
tendency in American film can be seen to permeate all of
his work (and many of his personal pronouncements as
well). [4]   In terms of opposition, it is also interesting to note
that while the New Wave was achieving many of its greatest
successes, Altman was deeply involved in that last bastion of
illusionist aesthetics--television production.

At this point, it should prove worthwhile to dip into
Altman's biography in an effort to round out his relationship
to both the European and American cinema.   He was born in
1925 in Kansas City, Missouri.   He was raised as a Roman
Catholic, and his early education took place in Jesuit schools.
He entered the army in 1943, at the age of eighteen, to become a B-24 bomber pilot in Southeast Asia.   Of these early
experiences, Altman has said: "Catholicism to me was school.
It was restrictions; it was things you had to do.   It was your
parents.   It was Mass on Sunday and fish on Friday.   And
then when I got out of that I got into the army.   It was the
same thing--you had to have a pass to get out. "[5]   When he
did get out, in 1947, Altman enrolled at the University of
Missouri, where he studied mathematical engineering.   Following that came a relatively unsuccessful period of writing
(for magazines, radio, and film), and six years of industrial
filmmaking in Kansas City.

In 1955, after receiving local backing, Altman produced, directed, and wrote his first feature film, The Delinquents, which was released in 1957.

> Well, this guy back there said he had the money
> to make a picture, if I'd make it about delinquents.
> I said OK and I wrote the thing in five days, cast
> it, picked the locations, drove the generator truck,
> got the people together, took no money, and we
> just did it, that's all.  My motives at that time
> were to make a picture, and if they said I gotta
> shoot it in green in order to get it done, I'd say,
> "Well, I can figure out a way to do that."  I would
> have done anything to get the thing done. 6

Made for $63,000, The Delinquents might be viewed today
as a low-budget version of Rebel Without a Cause, replete
with Tom (Billy Jack) Laughlin as the troubled young James
Dean-type hero whose major problems stem from the lack
of understanding manifested by "the older generation," and
the rowdy crowd of toughs with whom he hangs out.  I say
"might be viewed," because of the fact that since the film's
release, Altman has apparently gathered up most of the existing prints and has demonstrated a marked reluctance to
screening it.  "I'm not embarrassed about it," Altman has
said, "but nobody knew what they were doing.  I don't think
it has any meaning to anybody."7  Despite Altman's admoni-
tions, a brief summary of the film's plot, and a few critical
comments on his directorial execution, are in order here.

The Delinquents focuses upon a teenage love story involving Scotty (Laughlin) and Janice (Rosemary Howard), an
innocent young girl whose parents attempt to thwart her affair because they feel that she's "not ready to go steady" at
sweet sixteen.  Consequently, Scotty enlists the aid of one of
his greaser buddies (Peter Miller), who cleans himself up
and manages to pick up Janice and bring her to Scotty.  The
lovers meet at a teen party held at an abandoned mansion on
the outskirts of town.  The party gets out of hand, but the
lovers leave shortly before the police inexplicably arrive and
put an end to the bash.  Because they suspect Scotty of calling the cops, the toughs pick him up and make him an unwill-
ing scapegoat to an aborted filling station holdup.  Scotty gets
away, finds that Janice has been kidnapped by the gang,
tracks her down, and saves her after beating up the toughest
of the toughs (Miller).

Perhaps the most noteworthy aspect of The Delinquents

(in relationship to the bulk of Altman's work) is that it exhibits few if any of the innovative narrative structures and techniques upon which his reputation rests. Despite the high level of technical achievement evidenced by the film's superior use of lighting and the fine quality of its black-and-white cinematography, The Delinquents is best remembered as a lightweight nostalgic genre piece from the 1950s, a piece that nevertheless launched Altman's career. Finally, in addition to Laughlin's incredibly mannered performance, it is worth noting that the film is marred by a horrendous framing narration that utters such inanities as, "This story is about violence and immorality.... Who is to blame?... We are all responsible. "

Curiously enough, though Altman has stated that this narration was added at the insistence of his distributor (United Artists, to whom he sold the film for $150,000), his next film, The James Dean Story, features a similar device. A compiled documentary, The James Dean Story (1957) relies mainly on what the film's introduction terms "the dynamic exploration of the still photo" in a rather unsuccessful attempt to explore ("exploit" might be a more appropriate term) the life of the young man whose brief career ended so abruptly in 1955. This is not to say that Stewart Stern (who wrote Rebel) and coproducers and codirectors Altman and George W. George weren't genuinely interested in Dean, but that the film labors through a series of bland interviews with various relatives and friends with only an occasional film clip of Dean in action to liven up the pace. Moreover, instead of offering the viewer any real insight into Dean's life, Stern's narration drones on and on to the accompaniment of clichéd images (e. g., a dead seagull on the beach whose wasted potential is compared to the actor's).

Unless one is willing to overemphasize its painfully obvious theme and debatably "experimental" method of exposition, The James Dean Story merits even less discussion than The Delinquents in relationship to Altman's subsequent films. Nevertheless, the film apparently brought Altman to the attention of Alfred Hitchcock, who offered him a contract to direct for the Alfred Hitchcock Presents series at CBS. Altman opted to turn out only two episodes of his choice: The Young One (1957), and Together (1958). Between 1957 and 1963, Altman concentrated entirely on television, directing for such series as Bonanza, Bus Stop, Combat, Kraft Mystery Theater, and Kraft Suspense Theater. One of his longer Kraft Suspense Theater pieces, Nightmare in Chicago, was turned into a TV movie in 1964.

Then, in 1963, Altman and Ray Wagner formed a
partnership to do television and films.   They located in
Westwood (Los Angeles) and called their company Lion's
Gate Films.   Together they developed a film called Petulia,
among others, but had difficulty getting backing for the projects with Altman as the director.   Wagner eventually produced Petulia in 1967, with Richard Lester directing.   Meanwhile, after several years of virtual unemployment, Altman
directed his third film, Countdown, in 1966.   This finalized
Altman's break with TV production and marked his reentry
into the realm of feature filmmaking.   Countdown must be
viewed as an inauspicious reentry, however, due to the fact
that Altman was fired from the project at the editing stage.
According to Altman:

> Countdown was based on a book I'd tried to option
> for myself, Hank Searls's The Pilgrim Project,
> and I had a yen to do it.   I think we made a good
> little picture out of it--except for the editing,
> which was Jack Warner's idea.   With just a few
> days [of shooting] left, the old man asked to see
> an assemblage.   "Jesus Christ!" he said, "you've
> got all the actors talking at once!   Who's going to
> understand it?"   What Warner did was to cut the
> picture for kids.   Which is the reverse of what I
> was going for.   In theory, the film was about a
> moon shot; but what interested me was the human
> situation behind such endeavors:   the petty politics,
> the bitchiness of the wives, that sort of thing.   The
> cut Warner did played the obvious.   It became a
> lot of flag waving. [8]

This quotation raises several themes that will be returned to
again and again throughout this study.   The first has to do
with Altman's penchant for experimenting with overlapping
dialogue.   This technique, which he had begun to develop in
the late 1950s, was also the cause of several creative dis-
putes that marked his career in TV.   It is also indicative
of a strong formative desire to work against the traditional
expectations and conventions of genre.

The above also begins to provide an answer to the
question of why Altman left a financially rewarding career
in TV and began to gravitate toward independent production.
That is, in terms of what I have previously described as
his "inner-directedness," Altman's entire career can be seen
as an attempt to gain more and more personal control over

his creative material.   At the same time, this personal attitude cannot be separated from Altman's growing opposition
to traditional concepts of narration based on literary and
theatrical conventions.   More specifically, his directorial
progression indicates an unmistakable reaction against the
American television and film industry's preference for uni-
tive melodramatic patterns that encourage an attitude of passive acceptance on the part of the audience.   Altman's conception of film is analogous to his treatment of a long list
of filmic characters who are seen as possessing enormous
potential that is all too often thwarted by the constricting
forces of a herdlike society.   What I hope to demonstrate
in the pages that follow is that this does not amount to a
case of revolt for its own sake, but rather that alternatives
are offered in formal terms, or in the aspect of modernism
that encourages deep-rooted response and reflection.

   Altman's offhand comment that "I had done two pictures before Brewster McCloud really, " goes a long way
toward describing how important personal control over his
projects is to him.   In other words, after his two pre-TV
films and the release of a truncated version of Countdown
in 1968, That Cold Day in the Park (1969) is the first film
in which his still-formative creative vision was given more
or less free reign to surface.   In this context, it is interesting to note that when an interviewer asked Altman, in
1978, what he thought of his old films, he replies that "I
looked at A Cold Day in the Park recently, and I want to
tell you, that's one hell of a movie!"9   While he was cutting Cold Day, Altman became the fourteenth or fifteenth
(accounts vary) director approached by Ingo Preminger to
do M*A*S*H, the film that was to become his first international success.

   What remains to be done in this introduction is to
provide the reader with an outline or plan of this text.   Accordingly, I have divided it into three major sections, which
will focus upon "Themes and Structures, " "Genre and Myth,"
and the relationship between "Film and Dreams. "   The first
of these sections will concentrate on Altman's use of recurrent themes and techniques and the relationship of these elements to the concept of the "open text. "   This chapter will
also investigate the utility of this concept (the open text) as
a means of characterizing Altman's work, in conjunction with
specific analyses of M*A*S*H, California Split, Nashville,
and A Wedding.   "Genre and Myth" will attempt to distinguish
Altman's "personal" treatment of science fiction (Countdown,

Quintet), the western (McCabe and Mrs. Miller and Buffalo
Bill and the Indians), the gangster film (Thieves Like Us),
the detective film (The Long Goodbye), and the musical comedy (The Perfect Couple), from other approaches to these
generic forms.   Section three will discuss the relationship
between "Film and Dreams" (in general), through the specific analysis of the four Altman films that make the strongest use of dream modes as a method of narration (That Cold
Day in the Park, Brewster McCloud, Images, and Three
Women).

Finally, as this outline indicates, I do not intend to
argue for the sequential development of Altman's films.   In
other words, despite the fact that most of his works share
similar thematic elements and evince a constant effort on
Altman's part to refine certain specific techniques, his most
recent films do not necessarily represent a culmination of
earlier trends in qualitative terms.   Moreover, as Altman
himself has stated, "I know that once I've made a film, I
can't make the same kind of film right away."10   Consequently, an examination of his entire oeuvre can be seen to
reveal a sort of hopscotch pattern rather than a straightfor-
ward line of progression.   This pattern accounts for a great
deal of the apparently overlapping discussion (e. g. , both
dream modes and "personal" approaches to genre are in essence specific types of narrative techniques) in the chapters
that follow.


## NOTES


1"Sontag Talking, " an interview in The New York
Times Book Review, December 18, 1977, pp. 31-33.
2Arthur Koestler, The Act of Creation (New York:
Macmillan, 1964), p. 86.
3Ibid.
4In The Lonely Crowd:   A Study in the Changing
American Character, David Riesman distinguishes other-
directed people who demand security, and whose desires and
ambitions are oriented toward society, from the inner-directed
type, people who can cope with the confusion of a changing
society because they possess the self-discipline to drive
toward a goal that they have chosen themselves.
5"The Artist and the Multitude Are Natural Enemies, "
an interview in Film Heritage, Winter 1976-77, p. 18.

[6]Robert Altman, quoted in Todd McCarthy, "The Delinquents," in King of the B's, ed. Todd McCarthy and Charles Flynn (New York: Dutton, 1975), p. 216.

[7]Ibid.

[8]Robert Altman, quoted in Judith M. Kass, Robert Altman: American Innovator (New York: Popular Library, 1978), p. 51.

[9]An untitled interview in Film Comment, September-October 1978, p. 18.

[10]Ibid., p. 17.

# CHAPTER II

## THEMES AND STRUCTURES

I have already characterized Robert Altman as something of an "inner-directed" rebel who is prone to innovation and taking chances (he is also well known for his gambling). At the same time, Altman combines the seemingly incongruous qualities of the inveterate gambler with a remarkably consistent artistic vision. Thus, although only two of his last fifteen features (M*A*S*H and Nashville) have achieved real financial success, he has proved himself unique in his ability to keep making the kind of films that stimulate his audience's sense of meaning, without having to compromise that vision. In short, he is clearly a modernist survivor.

A very crucial aspect of Altman's work involves the ways in which his films can be considered to be "open," and how this quality of openness can encourage an "active" response. Before we begin to cite specific examples, however, it is important to state that the way themes and structures are employed at all levels of the films (i. e., thematic, dramatic, psychological, technical), is what really makes such a response worthy of our attention. Consequently, although the various elements involved can and will be broken down for purposes of analysis, we should not lose sight of the fact that it is the movement toward integration (the total perception of form) that we are ultimately trying to illuminate. If we begin with a general examination of narrative structures, we find that most of Altman's films avoid standard plots and traditional methods of character development. In this regard, Altman has continually relied upon a central technique that involves the use of ambiguous narrative structures, often achieved by what Koestler has referred to as the complementary techniques of "emphasis" and "economy." That is, by leaving various elements of plot and character development (which are usually explained) "open," Altman in effect is able to direct the burden of the riddle toward the viewer.

12

In the four films that make the strongest use of
dream modes (That Cold Day, Brewster McCloud, Images,
Three Women), for example, there is a constant tension between dreams or fantasy and everyday reality that is never
resolved by the director.   Moreover, it is this insistence
on Altman's part that there are no finite answers to such
questions that creates "logical gaps which the [viewer] has
to bridge by his own efforts. "   This also pinpoints the difference between Altman's strategy and that of the directors
of most mysteries, who answer their own riddles by inevitably letting us know "whodunit. "   In contrast, Altman's
"mysteries" are generally devoid of solutions.   This is because (bisociative) structures of ambiguity in a film like
That Cold Day in the Park can be seen to permeate the
movie's entire conception.

More specifically, that film creates an initial aura
of suspense through the use of "emphasis"--the protagonist
picks up a mysterious young man who is "apparently" mute,
though it is suggested that the young man may in fact be
putting on an act.   But rather than dwell on this method of
suggestion or attempt to incorporate it into "habit-formed
[narrative] channels, " Altman simply leaves us dangling for
an inexplicably long period of time.   This is one of the
many ways in which Altman compounds the conditions affect-
ing spectator interaction.   Not only have these suggestions
been spaced wide enough to "require a significant effort from
the receiver of the message, " but, simultaneously, the seemingly contradictory techniques of emphasis and economy are
operating at several other levels of the narrative, complicat-
ing the entire process.

The most important of these other levels has to do
with the lack of self-awareness manifested by Altman's protagonist (Frances/Sandy Dennis).   It is this very "lack" (or
"manqué") that both propels the action and implicates the
spectator in nearly all of Altman's works.   Brewster McCloud,
McCabe, Cathryn (Images), Marlowe, Wade (The Long Goodbye), the thieves, Bill, Charlie (California Split), Buffalo
Bill, and the three women are other characters who all fit
this pattern to some extent.   Taking a somewhat different
approach, Robin Wood has described "the most persistent
recurrent pattern in Altman's films--their basic auteurist
structure" in the following terms:   "The protagonist embarks
on an undertaking he is confident he can control; the sense
of control is progressively revealed as illusory; the protag-

onist is trapped in a course of events that culminates in disaster (frequently death). "1

However, although Wood's assessment is basically accurate, it fails to take into account the ways in which simultaneous fragmentation of narrative form and of the characters' egos may offer up the potential for the viewer to experience expanded fields of consciousness.  The above represents an equally important aspect of Altman's "auteurist
structure" that is all too often overlooked.  By bombarding
us with open-ended experiences on numerous levels, Altman's
films seek to undermine our own ego structures and induce
at least a temporary sense of another degree of awareness.
This strategy fits in well with the findings of R. D. Laing
and other humanist or existential psychologists who believe
that in breaking up the ego we experience other worlds and
other consciousnesses.  Of course, the effect of this strategy on the spectator will, as always, be dependent on both
the individual spectator involved and the ability of the filmmaker to bring it all off.  This last point, then, begs the
fundamental question of the aesthetics of consciousness.

In "The Empty Staircase and the Chinese Princess"
(Film Comment, September-October 1974), Michael Dempsey
has observed that one of the most persistent patterns in Altman's films involves the figure of the "dreamer" who, cut
off from the community, creates his or her own world of
fantasy.  Once again Brewster McCloud and Cathryn are
probably the most obvious of these figures, who include the
thieves, Marlowe and Wade, Buffalo Bill, the three women,
Essex (Quintet), and several minor characters from Nashville and A Wedding.  Hot Lips and the chief surgeon in
M*A*S*H are also dreamers, but of a somewhat different
nature.  Then, after noting that Altman is preoccupied "with
the destruction of humanity's most vulnerable members,"
Dempsey goes on to contrast these dreamers to Altman's
"hardnosed realists"--Suzanne and the cops in Brewster,
the various schemers in The Long Goodbye, Hugh in Images,
the heroes in M*A*S*H, and Mattie in Thieves Like Us.
Buffalo Bill, McCabe, Three Women, Nashville, A Wedding,
and Quintet are also peopled by realists whose most distinc-
tive traits conform to David Reisman's conception of the
"other-directed" type (i. e. , they are unable to transcend
their outwardly oriented goals and ambitions).

Dempsey doesn't push this contrast too far though,
because he feels that Altman's most "resonant" films are

those in which the lines of demarcation (between realist and dreamers) are the least rigid.   This last observation tends to oversimplify, however, as does Dempsey's assertion that the realists are usually mocked or satirized (except in M*A*S*H), while the dreamers inevitably fail ("there is no denying that Altman's dreamers generally end up dead or crazy").   This oversimplification may be due in part to the early date of Dempsey's essay, but in any event it is important to restate the fact that the ostensible failure of Altman's protagonists alluded to by both Dempsey and Wood does not necessarily undermine Altman's humanism.   For, even when there is no ambiguity surrounding the failure of these dreamers, a strong opposing force is generally implicit in Altman's films.   In terms of the "open spaces" that permeate them, this force encourages the viewer to reflect upon those factors that caused the "destruction" of these figures.   Moreover, because these factors invariably indict a social system that is seen to be restrictively artless and barren (and in this sense the cause of the lack of self-awareness manifested by the protagonist), another dialectic is apparent.

Again, this tendency in Altman's work shares many points of contact with R. D. Laing's statement in The Politics of Experience that "the condition of alienation, of being asleep, of being unconscious, of being out of one's mind, is the condition of the normal man. "  In accordance with Altman's inverted structure, then, it is society at large that is seen to be sick, inasmuch as it denies individuals the right to express their inner-directed aspirations.   This is not meant to suggest that Altman favors his dreamers without reservations, but rather that he himself can be seen as a "realistic dreamer" who is aware of the need to integrate both aspects within the individual.   Bearing this in mind, we will see that it is only Altman's nonintegrated dreamers who are destroyed.

Looking over Altman's entire oeuvre, we find a marked variance in terms of both artistic quality and resonance (the ability to stimulate meaningful audience interaction).   But although these qualitative differences are sometimes a result of overly rigid thematic oppositions, there are other explanations.   According to Robin Wood, much of this variance can be attributed to those personal techniques that he has labeled "smart-ass and cutie-pie" (the phrase comes from a discussion in The Long Goodbye):

Presumably the "smart-ass" antagonizes while the

"cutie-pie" seeks to disarm, but both use slickness
or cleverness as a defense and an evasion.  They
express at once an assertion that one is in control
and an inadvertent admission (because of their
transparent inadequacy) that one is not....  His
films are successful in direct ratio to the degree
to which the smart-ass element is assimilated and
"placed" within the narrative structure, dramatized
in the leading character (McCabe, Marlowe) and revealed as the inadequate defense of a very vulnerable man. 2

   For Wood, these smart-ass elements are exemplified
by Altman's "smug" treatment of sex (M*A*S*H, That Cold
Day in the Park--and I'm sure he would include Buffalo Bill
and A Wedding), the use of ungrounded "gimmicks" (M*A*S*H,
Brewster McCloud, Images, The Long Goodbye, Thieves Like
Us, Nashville), and overworked caricatures (M*A*S*H, Nashville, A Wedding).  More specifically, in Thieves and Nashville (to select but two brief examples), these elements are
insistently forced upon the viewer.  With regard to Thieves,
Wood cites the use of the radio announcer who punctuates
Bowie and Keechie's lovemaking by proclaiming, "Thus did
Romeo and Juliet consummate their first interview by falling
madly in love with each other. "  The essence of Wood's
point is that this potentially ironic device is not used once
(because "Altman can't leave well enough alone"), but three
times!  In reference to Nashville, Wood states that the
film's "central failure lies in the Geraldine Chaplin figure. "
The rationale behind this judgment is that this "outsider-
interviewer" is the only character in the film with sufficient
distance to make sense out of (or to help the audience make
sense out of) "the moral and emotional confusion in which
everyone else is trapped.... "  Thus, Wood feels that Altman has squandered this potential by making Chaplin appear
to be "as idiotic as he can. "

   While this last observation will be questioned shortly,
there is no doubt that Altman's repeated use of similar techniques often constitutes an apparently unmotivated flaunting of
the filmmaker's own ego.  Another striking example of this
occurs in Quintet, just after Deuca's death.  In this scene,
Deuca is placed in the middle of the frame for what seems
like an interminable period of time, with a spike stuck through
her head.  The effect is almost comical (in a smart-ass
sense) due to the length of time that Altman stays with the
shot.  Consequently, when Ambrosia (Bibi Andersson) finally

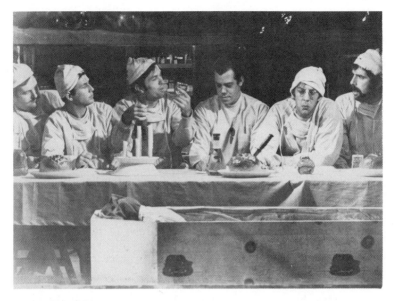

From M*A*S*H

covers Deuca with a cloak, it is almost as if Altman is saying, "I could have done this sooner, but I'd rather see you
[the audience] squirm. "

## M*A*S*H (1970)

There are a variety of reasons why it is only slightly
ironic that Altman's most commercially successful film to
date--M*A*S*H--is also the one in which his smart-ass tendencies are the most dominant.   Topping the list is the idea
that while the kind of open-endedness that we have been dis-
cussing is not necessarily antithetical to the production of
commercially viable "products, " in point of fact, the two
have seldom meshed (especially in the U. S. ).   The other
reasons stem from the fact that with M*A*S*H, Altman was
dealing with a preconceived property that differs from the
bulk of his source materials in several fundamental ways.
In addition to his being way down on the list of directors to
whom producer Ingo Preminger showed the Ring Lardner,
Jr. , script (based on the novel by Richard Hooker), M*A*S*H

is the only Altman film in which the "realists" are unequiv-
ocally extolled.  Thus, it is both the very nature of the
source materials, and the reversal of Altman's (still formative) "basic auteurist structure" governed by these sources,
that makes M*A*S*H an exception in the director's oeuvre.

On the other hand, M*A*S*H is crammed full of the
kind of techniques upon which a large measure of Altman's
reputation rests.  These techniques include his use of actors, sound, editing, and the moving camera.  Thematically,
M*A*S*H shows similarities to many of Altman's other works
in its treatment of madness in relationship to the quest for
some kind of community.  It is also unconventionally plotted,
and, like Nashville, Buffalo Bill, and A Wedding, it deals
with an unusually large number of major characters within a
tightly circumscribed space and time.  M*A*S*H's major
problem, however, is that the very nature of the "open
spaces" involved (i. e. , the way they are integrated with
themes and structures) can be seen to preclude a potentially
"expanding" response.

If we begin the multifaceted explanation of these relative strengths and weaknesses by placing M*A*S*H in some
historical perspective, we find that it has many affinities
with the subgenre of antiwar comedies, which includes
films like Catch-22, Oh, What a Lovely War, Dr. Strange-
love, How I Won the War, and Stalag 17.  Among these,
Catch-22 was released in the same year as M*A*S*H (1970),
while Stalag 17 was used as the basis (like M*A*S*H) for a
TV show (Hogan's Heroes).  Catch-22 in particular bears
many similarities to M*A*S*H, inasmuch as both of these
novel-derived American productions were released at a time
when anti-Vietnam sentiment was running very high in this
country.  Despite their being set in earlier wars, each of
these films also uses madness as a central motif to comment upon the contemporary situation.  Of the two, however,
M*A*S*H has a much looser plot and a greater density on
the audiovisual level.  One of the main reasons for this difference is that M*A*S*H's "catch-22" does not involve the
threat of physical danger to its protagonists.  Consequently,
unlike Catch-22, it contains no real crisis structure.

Like the Hooker novel, Altman's M*A*S*H is made
up of a series of predominantly comic episodes that make
little or no attempt to build conflict in a traditional sense
(i. e. , there is limited rising action, no obligatory scene or
cathartic climax, etc. )  Moreover, the conflicts that do exist

are resolved at a relatively early stage.    The main area in
which the film and novel do differ, however, involves their
respective methods of exposition.    The opening sequences of
both versions provide us with several key indications of the
nature of this contrast.

To begin with, the fact that the novel informs us
about the meaning of its title (Mobile Army Surgical Hospital) on page one, while the film never does get around to
revealing this information, is a good deal more significant
than one might at first think.    The novel is prone to "explaining" action, events, and characters to a much greater
extent than the film is.    The introduction of the character
known as Radar O'Reilly is another case in point.    Hooker
actually begins his novel with a description of Radar's
"unique extrasensory powers."    In many ways a unifying
force in both versions, it is through Radar's already explained ability to overhear Colonel Blake's phone conversation that the personnel of the 4077th M. A. S. H. learn that
two new "chest-cutters" are about to join them.

Because of the way in which this knowledge is trans-
mitted, the book's opening transition is very smoothly accomplished.    Accordingly, we glide right into the introduction of the two new surgeons, Hawkeye and Duke (Donald
Sutherland and Tom Skerritt), secure in our knowledge that
they are on their way.    This feeling of security is further
augmented by dialogue and description.    We immediately
learn that they (and M*A*S*H, by implication) have a sense
of humor, and that Hawkeye is a little "nuts."    We find out
where they're from, and how Hawkeye got his name.    And,
most important of all, we are told that their colleagues ad-
mired their professional zeal and efficiency but were somewhat mystified by their overwhelming irreverence.

In contrast, the film offers us many similar "impressions" in its opening scenes, but shows a marked reluctance
to fill in certain kinds of detail.    In its more visceral approach, Altman's M*A*S*H opens (over credits) with moving
camera shots of army helicopters delivering their cargos of
wounded soldiers.    On the sound track, a ballad ("Suicide Is
Painless") sets the tone of the film but is soon replaced by
the sound of helicopters.    Following the opening credits, the
camera zooms in on Radar O'Reilly (Gary Burghoff), who is
engaged in a conversation that is unintelligible because of the
way that overlapping dialogue is mixed with wild sound.    Our
only clue to what is happening (and to Radar's "talent") comes

when a third enlisted man asks the colonel what he was saying to Radar and is told that "Radar knows what he needs to
know." Consequently, we are totally unprepared for the next
show, which begins with a titled excerpt from MacArthur's
farewell address, unraveling itself over Hawkeye's first actions. However, if we are still in doubt as to the irony of
this superimposition (i.e., Hawkeye as "the fighting son,
splendid in every way"), Hawkeye's behavior quickly sets us
straight. That is, he steals a jeep while posing as Duke's
driver, and takes off with a bottle of booze in one hand and
the steering wheel in the other.

Arriving at the 4077th, the camera zooms into a
close-up of Lieutenant Dish (Jo Ann Pflug), shot from Duke's
point of view. Together with the speed with which Duke
makes his play for Lt. Dish, it is this privileged (because
it is subjective) shot that marks him off as one of our "heroes." At least that is our impression. Similarly, the
rapid-fire series of introductions of M*A*S*H's leading characters that ensues gives us the impression of a rather zany
community. This feeling is further reinforced by the use of
overlapping dialogue and an equally persistent barrage of non-
sense emanating from the P.A. Even the Colonel seems to
fit right in, as he orders the plates changed on the jeep that
he knows to be stolen.

This is how the movie works. As compared with the
novel, transitions are extremely abrupt, and we never really
learn about the background and function of many of the leading characters. What we do get are impressions--impres-
sions of a nonordinary community in which all the members
seem to accept the fact that they must be a little crazy in
order to survive. In other words, because Altman is dealing with an atypical situation (the war), madness has become
a pragmatic means of survival. Essentially, it is this thematic inversion that makes M*A*S*H so different from Altman's other films, by reversing the usual function of his
"realists" and "dreamers."

By the same token, this inversion also hints at the
main structural weakness of the film, inasmuch as the deck
is so cleverly stacked from the start. For, whereas Altman's strong suit has invariably involved his sympathetic
treatment of "humanity's most vulnerable members,"
M*A*S*H manifests an inordinate lack of compassion. Thus,
while survival maintains its status as a repeatedly crucial
goal, the character complexities that make it worth fighting

from which to zoom in (through a window) to a close-up of
Burns, who is dictating a letter of complaint to his new-
found cohort.   Here, again, it is the overtness of the zoom
that makes it worthy of our consideration.   For, although
Altman has undoubtedly been more successful in integrating
this device into the overall structure of many of his other
films (That Cold Day, The Long Goodbye, Three Women),
this particular shot serves to illustrate its expressive potential.   In addition to its calling attention to the presence of
the director, Altman's use of the zoom virtually reverses
that variety of realism associated with deep focus. [3]   This
is accomplished by the control that the zoom exerts over the
spectator's gaze.   Also, despite the fact that M*A*S*H tends
to favor the kind of highly visible cutting patterns referred
to above in lieu of more zooms, it should be noted that this
latter device has an even greater ability to "dissolve space
and undermine our sense of physical reality."[4]   However,
in the present instance, because the creation of such structural uncertainty conflicts with the far-from-ambiguous characterizations and motivations of Hot Lips and Burns, Altman's (and cinematographer Harold E. Stine's) zoom is reduced to just another bravura stroke of the camera.

  Another aspect of this shot that bears mentioning is
Altman's use of the plastic window, inasmuch as reflective
surfaces (glass, mirrors, water) frequently appear in conjunction with the director's zooms. [5]

  To get back to the action at hand:   Burns leaves Hot
Lips after a passionate embrace, and promises to check on
her later that evening.   In the following scene, the two hypo-
critical dreamers go so far as to invoke God's name to sanc-
tion their illicit affair (Burns is married). Burns (frothing at
the mouth):   "God meant us to be together."   Hot Lips (opening her robe):   "His will be done."

  It is at this point that a shift in camera angle reveals
several of the men spying on the couple from behind an un-
shaded window.   Moments later, Radar, at Trapper's instigation, places a P.A. mike under Hot Lips's cot, and the entire company is made privy to their outrageous intimacies
(this is where "Hot Lips" gets her name).   Hearing their
own echoing voices, Hot Lips and Burns jump up in frantic
confusion as the scene ends.

  The next day is Burns's last in the camp.   But despite his undeniable failings as both a surgeon and a human

being, the way in which he is ultimately dispatched is somewhat disturbing.   Hawkeye baits Burns at the breakfast table,
fully aware that the recently returned Colonel Blake is watching them through the window.   Burns freaks out, attacks
Hawkeye, and is next seen exiting the camp in a straitjacket
as the P. A. blares "Sayonara. "   My objections do not concern the outcome (Burns obviously has to go), but rather the
glib manner in which we are encouraged to laugh it all off,
for, as culpable as Burns is, the method of his elimination
is symptomatic of a considerably less obvious hypocrisy on
the part of the filmmakers.   This has been summed up well
be Roger Greenspun's comment that "M*A*S*H accepts without question several current pieties (for example, concern
for a child's life, but not a grown man's soul).... "6

A similar criticism could be leveled at M*A*S*H's
treatment of Painless Pole's "problem. "   Although, in this
instance, the community acts with compassion, the entire
episode is tainted by its smart-ass premise.   In brief, the
episode revolves around the Pole's mistaken assumption that
he's "a fairy" ("a victim of latent homosexuality"), and the
group's efforts to thwart his resultant suicide attempt.   In
typical Altman fashion, the Pole's "last supper" begins with
a horizontal camera movement before slowly zooming in on
Painless, who is being prepared by Trapper, the inverted
Judas.   A light bulb (halo) has been strategically placed over
the Christ-figure's head and a mock dirge ("Suicide Is Painless") is sung while the Pole swallows his "black capsule. "
As the men file by the coffin, Altman cuts to a conversation
between Hawkeye and Lieutenant Dish in which Hawkeye
cleverly suggests that she take care of Painless, for "thera-
peutic" purposes.   This, in turn, is accomplished as Dish
joins Painless on his bier (to the tune of Hollywood strings
and a choral accompaniment), which is bathed in soft red
light.   By morning, Painless is his old self, and Dish flies
out of camp with a smile of fulfillment on her face.

Sandwiched as it is between Burns's victimization and
Hot Lips's subsequent humiliation in the shower, this "last
supper" sequence plays like an apparent attempt to mitigate
against our sense of the community's callousness.   But, like
that episode in which Hawkeye and Trapper go to great
lengths to operate on a fatherless baby in Japan, it is marred
by its childish sense of sanctimony.   Moreover, Altman's
smirking use of homosexuality as a butt for his humor cannot
be condoned in terms of his source materials, as it crops up
in at least several other of his films (That Cold Day, A Wed-

ding).   Overall, it is this impulse to go for easy laughs at the expense of both thematic and character consistency that proves to be M*A*S*H's most glaring flaw.

The way that M*A*S*H deals with Hot Lips is another case in point.   After "the last supper," Duke bets Hawkeye that Hot Lips is not a natural blond.   In order to settle the bet, the men rig her shower curtains in what amounts to yet another voyeuristic display.   At her wits' end, she runs off to Colonel Blake's tent and threatens to resign.   Relaxing in his bed in the company of an attractive young nurse, the colonel could care less.   Thus far, Hot Lips would seem to be headed for the same ignominious fate that overtook Burns, but rather than bring this conflict to some kind (any kind) of fruition, Altman simply lets it drop out of sight.   Accordingly, when next we see Hot Lips (following Hawkeye and Trapper's escapades in Japan), she has just gotten out of the sack with Duke.   And not only does this extreme turn of events remain unexplained, but this one brief scene serves as the only bridge between Hot Lips's function as the company's chief antagonist and its head cheerleader.

M*A*S*H is at its best when both its humor and more serious elements seem to be the most spontaneous or un-forced.   The colonel's fishing, Hawkeye and Trapper's golf game on the landing strip, Hawkeye's pose for an American moviemaker, and several of the operating scenes all fit the bill to varying degrees.   Equally impressive is the ambiance of many of the ensemble scenes brought about by the film-maker's skillful use of actors, sound, and moving camera.

M*A*S*H is also noteworthy as the first Altman film to introduce a wide-ranging group of performers, many of whom have gone on to reinforce his communal themes through their reappearance in subsequent Altman films.   Elliott Gould, Tom Skerritt, Sally Kellerman, Rene Auberjonois, John Schuck, Bud Cort, David Arkin (Vollmer), and G. Wood (Gen-eral Hammond) are all members of this soon-to-be-expanded (and ever shifting) "repertory" contingent, as are Robert Du-vall and Michael Murphy (Me Lay), both of whom appeared in previous Altman films.   Among these, Elliott Gould's per-formance particularly stands out for its easy-going sense of spontaneity, a factor that undoubtedly influenced Altman's casting of Gould in his most improvised effort, California Split.

The latter part of M*A*S*H, however, suffers from

its inclination to unduly force its precarious sense of humor.
This is exemplified by both Hawkeye and Trapper's Japanese
adventure and the culminating football game.  The football
sequence is especially revealing, inasmuch as it utilizes nearly every gag in the comic canon in a rather desperate attempt
to provoke our laughter.  The token motivation that exists for
the game (which is more than can be said for the Japanese
episode) comes when General Hammond arrives to take up a
complaint lodged by Hot Lips.  Thus, when the general casually mentions that his company's team plays other outfits
for a sizable pot, Hawkeye's ears perk up because he knows
of a "ringer" who's stationed with a nearby unit.  Then, in
rapid order, Hawkeye has the colonel set up the confrontation, "Spearchucker" arrives, a team is fielded, with Colonel
Blake as the nominal coach, and the game begins.

    The rest of the sequence fails to make the grade be-
cause it relies on an overabundance of isolated comic devices
at a point in the film that demands a greater sense of rising
action.  That is, even if we have come to accept the film's
episodic structure, the ensuing series of sight gags and verbal quips is enough to tax our patience in view of the steady
diet of hi-jinx to which we have already been exposed.  Besides, the game itself is handled in a relatively conventional
manner, drawing on elements that date back to Harold Lloyd's
football farce in The Freshman (1925).  There are several
notable exceptions, however, including Hot Lips's cheers
("He's hurt, he's hurt, he's leaving the game 'cause he's
hurt"), and her reaction to the gun that ends the third quarter ("My God, they've shot him").  But on the whole, the
action is predictable and the humor soon begins to wear thin.

    Back at the camp, it's life as usual (poker games,
P.A. announcements, tending to the wounded) until Hawkeye
tells Duke that they're being sent home.  At this point, the
film simply takes the easy way out by opting for a self-
reflexive finish, in lieu of any thematic resolution.  Accordingly, after a zoom into the P.A. speaker, the announcer
tells us that "Tonight's movie has been M*A*S*H.  Follow
the zany antics of our combat surgeons as they cut and stitch
their way along the front lines."  Then, following a tracking
shot of Hawkeye and Duke pulling away in a jeep, the performers are identified in brief cameos before the announcer
signs off.

    If we now return to the question of the kind of re-
sponse that M*A*S*H's narrative techniques encourage, it is

From California Split

quite clear that the use of self-reflexivity in this instance
(or any isolated modernist technique for that matter) offers
no guarantee against closure.   Moreover, given Altman's
penchant for downplaying many of his successes, his comment that the film is "just a series of dirty jokes" that appeals to "the lowest common denominator" rings true in
many respects.

## California Split (1974)

Together with M*A*S*H, California Split (1974),
Nashville (1975), A Wedding (1978), and the upcoming Health
stand apart from Altman's other films in their refusal to be
easily categorized in terms of genre or dream modes.   However, these films can also be advantageously studied as a
unit for reasons other than their failure to conform to these
categories.   For example, M*A*S*H, Nashville, and A Wedding all deal with an increasingly large number of major
characters, a more and more tightly circumscribed physical
space, and progressively shorter time spans.   California

Split, on the other hand, is a "smaller" film that fits in here by virtue of the fact that Altman envisioned it, in part, as a testing ground for many of the more grandly structured techniques (especially those having to do with sound) he was planning to use in Nashville. All four of these films are also among Altman's least traditional works in terms of narrative conventions.

Although I have written at some length about personal signatures as one way in which directors can interject a sense of the "self" into their films, there are times when this concept can be easily overworked. One such instance has to do with Altman's use of sound. While overlapping dialogue is one of the few techniques that we can accurately talk about in terms of development, the primary goal of that development has been to achieve greater verisimilitude. In other words, Altman's "experiments" with overlapping dialogue can be seen, in Altman's own words, as an ongoing attempt "to improve the sound in order to create the illusion of reality." Thus, in the majority of his films, the structural use of sound, in terms of overlapping dialogue, exemplifies an impulse toward naturalism, which is then counterposed to various other less lifelike elements (i. e. , nonconventional plots, visual style, and editing). Moreover, in many of those cases, particularly among those films that pre-date California Split, in which overlapping dialogue has been singled out by critics, the "signature" is an unintentional one precisely because it calls undue attention to itself. Accordingly, as Altman has said, sound must be looked upon as "an integral part of the motion picture process." The following excerpt from a recent interview serves to bring home my point:

> INT:  There seems to be less overlapping dialogue [in A Wedding].
>
> ALT:  There's more overlapping dialogue in A Wedding than in any picture I've done!
>
> INT:  Maybe we've gotten used to you.
>
> ALT:  Maybe we're doing our sound a little better.[7]

One of the main reasons that Altman has been able to do his sound a little better since California Split involves the use of the Lion's Gate Eight-Track System, which was first employed on that film. Invented by Jac Cashin of Lion's

Gate and John Stephens of Stephens Electronics, it is described by Charles Schreger as follows:

> The key difference in the eight-track system is that
> each actor, instead of speaking into an overhead
> boom microphone (which picks up all the sound in
> a scene: the noise of the location as well as the
> voices of the performers), is equipped with a tiny
> radio mike, and speaks into it. There are no
> wires or cables; the sound is broadcast from the
> mike to a receiving unit. Each performer gets
> one channel, and the sound is individually controlled.
> For technical reasons, one channel must be elimi-
> nated; so, under the eight-track system, seven
> actors can speak at once. A separate recording
> unit picks up the background noise. [8]

According to Altman's long-time directorial assistant, Tommy
Thompson, "The radio mikes also allow him [Altman] the
freedom to not be confined to where the boom will reach.
You know the old joke, be sure and talk into the moosehead.
You don't have to do that any more. You can ignore the
moose entirely." As Schreger notes, this "freedom" is also
conducive to improvisation since the actors aren't tied down
to their marks. Moreover, one actor can interrupt another
without the director "working out complicated cues with the
boom operator."

In California Split, sound is just one of the major
elements used by Altman to create an "impression" of improvisation that underlies the film's main thematic concerns,
but it is because these very concerns also involve improvisation as a virtual lifestyle (which is given substance by the
central gambling motif) that is neither morally condoned nor
denigrated by the director, that California Split can be ex-
amined in the context of "open spaces."

> The difference, in short, between conventional
> methods and Altman's is one between directness
> and indirectness, actions and interactions--the
> actors', the characters', the director's, the script-
> writer's and our own. It is decidedly a group en-
> deavour, and as such, one that lives and breathes
> in an intangible no-man's-land between "thinking"
> and "playing" for the film-makers, "thinking" and
> spontaneous "reacting" for the audience; the rela-
> tive strengths of both values are held in perpetual

suspension, with new stimuli that can potentially
shift the balance coming along at every juncture.
From this point of view, anything can affect everything, and no two spectators are responding to precisely the same film--the complete "text" is common to all, but each reading of it varies according
to attentiveness, temperament and perceptual capacity:  an individual selection of what is interesting
or relevant and what is not. [9]

Due in part to its "experimental" underpinnings, however, it is doubtful whether California Split can be seen to
integrate its most "interesting" and "relevant" aspects in such
a way as to induce the kind of response that is truly "synergistic" (interactive, or acting together).  Nor does it really
attempt to do so.  California Split, more than any other of
Altman's films, fulfills the director's stated intention of en-
listing an "emotional" response rather than an intellectual
one:

> I try to allow each individual to actually see and
> experience a different film.  The attempt is to
> enlist an audience emotionally, not intellectually.
> I don't want anybody to come out with the right
> answer, 'cause I don't think there's any right
> answer....  What I want to do is get to the point
> where I think an audience can see a film, finish
> it, have an emotional response to it, and say noth-
> ing about it, not be able to articulate. [10]

But, by the same token, this quote--which reads like something out of Susan Sontag's Against Interpretation--simply
does not ring true when it is applied to most of Altman's
other works.  If the spectator's inability to "articulate" a
response was what Altman was really striving for, then, in
view of the enormous amount of "ink" that has been devoted
to his films, he would have to be considered an out-and-out
failure rather than one of the most critically acclaimed (and
thought-provoking) directors working in America today.

Contrary to Altman's statement, it is my contention
that the critical success of most of his films can be attributed to their post-factor ability to sustain the widest possible
variety of intellectual reflection.  While I fully agree that
there are no "right answers" to his films, it must be noted
that this very assertion is one that is arrived at through in-
tellection--just as criticism, by its very nature, can be none

other than an intellectual activity.   My point harkens back
to the Lawrencian notion of "inter-relatedness." That is,
even if Altman is consciously trying to enlist an emotional
response, I would argue that a concomitant intellectual response, in view of the specific nature of his themes and
structure, is part and parcel of Altman's (subconscious)
narrative strategies.   However, the crucial issue here is
not whether Altman's emotional and intellectual thrusts are
either consciously or subconsciously motivated, but, rather,
how successfully they are structured with the total form of
his films.   Again I use "intellectual," in this case to desig-
nate the way we reflect on various aspects of the spectacles--
one aspect of which involves our emotional response.

In other words (and I believe this accounts for Altman's
statement), Altman is justified in condemning certain types of
intellectual excesses (i. e. , overinterpretation), but, at the
same time, this should not be misconstrued as applying to
criticism as a whole.   Thus, while it may be true that Altman's quotation reveals an insecurity about, or defense
mechanism against, the possible intellectual failing of certain
of his films, I see it as an intuitive artist's reaction to the
persistent attempts to "decode" his messages, attempts that
all too often supersede the more viable practice of trying to
ascertain the meaning of the codes he has chosen.   Accordingly, the kind of external problems that I have been dis-
cussing can be seen to be created by the failure to make
certain distinctions (i. e. , Altman's failure--although, after
all, he's not a critic--to differentiate various kinds of intellectual responses).   Conversely, internal problems in the
films are created by Altman's failure to integrate all the
cinematic levels (dramatic, thematic, sound, visual, kinetic)
within a particular structure capable of eliciting a synergistic
response.   In fact, if this overall formal goal is ultimately
achieved, it will result in the kind of streamlined communi-
cation that Altman has, albeit incompletely, endeavored to
describe in terms of an "emotional" response.

Of course, there are still other potential levels of
response, some of which California Split in particular may
serve to exemplify.   The main reason for this is that not
only does California Split present a series of situations that
Altman refrains from commenting on in a judgmental or
moral sense (cf. "right answers"), but there is no real
thematic conflict to which the viewer may address either
thoughts or emotions.   In this respect, it is unlike any of
Altman's other films, all of which play upon some form of

thematic tension, no matter how obliquely.   This is not to
say that California Split is devoid of open spaces, but rather
that it is devoid of the kind of open spaces that one might
expect from Altman.   For, instead of providing us with either
his "typical auteurist structure" or the more expansive structural patterns of Nashville and A Wedding--both of which make
use of implicit attitudes toward society to add resonance to
Altman's open spaces--California Split plays an entirely different sort of game.   Like gambling (and gamblers), which
it ostensibly celebrates, the film cuts itself off from the
world at large by functioning in accordance with another set
of rules.

        Again, those roles are dictated in part by the film's
basis as an "etude" for future works.   But beyond its experiments with sound and improvisation, California Split marks
itself off from the rest of Altman's oeuvre by its steadfast
avoidance of even the most indirect kind of social commentary.   Because the film is about gambling, it is fitting that
Altman should emphasize the elements of chance and play,
which figure in so many of his works.   But in California
Split, they are the film's main raison d'être.   Unlike most
films that deal with this subject, however, there is no attempt to turn gambling into a microcosm or metaphor for
life (although the case could easily be made that gambling
does serve as a loose metaphor for Altman's filmmaking
methods).

        Both literally and figuratively, Altman is a gambler
who is every bit as obsessed with filmmaking as the protagonists of California Split are with games of chance.   Where
the comparison breaks down, however, is in the amount of
control that Altman exerts over the kind of risks he takes.
In this instance, those risks involve "not making a moral
judgment.   It [California Split] simply mirrors the atmosphere and the kind of world that gamblers function in."
Consequently, because California Split's freewheeling premise lacks any substantial core of ideas (which might generate conflict and tension), the odds seem to be stacked against
Altman from the start.   For even though this "open" situation would appear to provide Altman with the kind of chal-
lenge upon which his talents thrive, California Split fails to
provide the viewer with the kind of intellectual and emotional payoffs that make the traditional game of movie-going
worth playing.

        In typical fashion, however, Altman's answer to this

dilemma is simply to change the rules of the game.  In
other words, California Split is Altman's gamble that he can
take a series of loosely articulated situations, which defy
most of the rules of dramatic construction, and transform
them into an effective cinematic experience.   Of course,
this in itself is not an uncommon procedure for Altman.
But what does make California Split unique in comparison
with his other films is the way that notions of chance and
play take precedence over more weighty thematic concerns.
For example, whereas themes of insanity or obsession are
usually connected with "dreamers" whose individualistic visions are somehow frustrated by societal forces (Brewster
McCloud, McCabe, the thieves, etc.), the protagonists of
California Split have no real vision beyond their obsessions
with gambling and chance.   Similarly, in structural terms,
this lack of thematic tension leads to the creation of open
spaces in which the element of the "riddle" is subsumed by
the very same forces of chance that propel the protagonists.
Accordingly, what enables California Split to attain a level
of formal virtuosity that belies its apparently haphazard ve-
neer is Altman's ability to structure what appear to be a
series of improvisational situations and chance occurrences
into a tightly integrated whole.   The resultant payoff for the
spectator is that the stakes of the game are reduced to a
level at which it can be played strictly for fun.   The viewer
is absolved of the burden of the riddle, because open spaces
ruled by chance transform the very nature of the choices
that he or she must make.

  Although screenwriter Joseph Walsh's story line (what
Altman refers to as a "linear sequence") is typically loose
and rambling, Altman and Walsh counteract this impression
by employing several unifying devices that sharpen California
Split's focus.   The first of these devices has to do with the
way the film concentrates on its two protagonists, Charlie
Waters (Elliott Gould) and Bill Denny (George Segal).   Rather
than dispersing its energy among a long list of characters (as
in M*A*S*H, Nashville, and A Wedding), California Split's
predominant sense of organization is dependent on the various
associations woven into the contrast, or "split," between
Charlie and Bill.   The other major unifying device is provided by the obsessive behavior of these two characters,
which permeates the film.

  California Split prefaces the development of these devices with an opening sequence that simultaneously sets the
scene and makes its own ironic comment on the relationship

of gambling and the filmmaking process.   Thus, after the
apparently unacquainted Charlie and Bill cross paths amidst
the hubbub of a California casino, Charlie casually activates
a machine that begins to spew forth a "service" film on the
ins and outs of gambling.   Shortly thereafter, as the narrator's explanations in this film-within-a-film begin to conflict
with the actual occurrences with which they are intercut, we
begin to get the feeling that Altman has employed this self-
reflexive device to demonstrate the fact that California Split
will explore the world of gambling according to its own set
of rules.   This is particularly evident when Charlie's garrulous
poker ploys are played off against the narrator's comments
on "good table manners."   Moreover, when Charlie wins a
big hand largely because he has successfully managed to cir-
cumvent the rules of the game, Altman's subtle implication
is that California Split will attempt to achieve its cinematic
goals in a similar manner.

        This introductory sequence is also noteworthy for the
way in which it links Bill to Charlie.   For it is Bill, the
quiet and intense amateur, who backs Charlie up when he is
accused of cheating.   This results in a further accusation
that Bill and Charlie are in cahoots--a distinct possibility
that Altman purposely leaves open until the next sequence.
Finally, while Charlie characteristically talks his way out of
the ensuing hassle, Bill makes his silent getaway unseen, by
crawling across the floor of the casino.   It should also be
mentioned that while Bill is technically an amateur (he holds
down a "regular" job), the fact that he was recognized earlier by the casino's pit boss establishes the fact that he is
every bit as much of a habitué as Charlie is.

        The next scene clarifies Charlie's and Bill's relation-
ship.   They meet by chance in a darkened bar, where they
soon find that they hit it off together.   They get drunk, improvise a duet, and wind up their rendezvous with a half-
hearted, but inevitable, bet that Charlie won't be able to
name the seven dwarfs.   At the same time, Altman has dis-
played his own allegiance to chance (or "play") by fragmenting their obvious improvisations with the equally off-the-cuff
ramblings of a pair of gogo dancers.   Along with the many
chance meetings and occurrences that govern its linear sequence, it is this tendency to riddle California Split's surface with apparently improvised behavior that gives the viewer the initial impression that the film is as unstructured as
the lives of its protagonists.   As we come to know Bill and
Charlie better, however, we begin to realize that both their

mutual obsession and shared relationship are very definite
elements of structure.

After they are mugged by the sore loser from the
casino, the twosome is bailed out of jail by the pair of call
girls with whom Charlie shares his apartment.   At this
point, it is interesting to note that the beating they take can
be read as a direct result of their new-found friendship, inasmuch as Bill's and Charlie's behavior together confirms
the suspicions of their attacker.   Add to this the moral tur-
pitude of their present situation, and the future would seem
to be anything but good.   After all, what kind of fortune can
we predict for a couple of beat-up gamblers who bed down
at dawn while one of their hooker friends eats Fruit Loops
for breakfast?  In point of fact, however, we don't know
what to predict, precisely because Altman's deceptively simple narrative strategy has already conditioned us to expect
the unexpected.   That is, by concentrating on the eccentric
attitudes and behavior of his characters in lieu of a more
standard plot, Altman has reprogrammed our narrative interactions and expectations.   What matters most is not what
these people are going to do in the future or why, but how
they react to the moment.   This is one of the more crucial
factors in Altman's amoral catalog of behaviors.

The sequence that follows this "morning after" scene
provides us with a striking example of the ways in which
Altman's concern with improvised surface behavior substitutes for more traditional narrative development.   Bill calls
Charlie from his office to tell him that he can't make it to
the racetrack.   On the bus to the track, Charlie engineers
a complicated scheme for changing seats, at the instigation
of a superstitious horseplayer (Barbara London), whom he
proceeds to "talk off" the longshot she is planning to bet.
At the track, however, when Charlie tells Barbara that she
might be right about "Egyptian Femme," she has already
been dissuaded.   Meanwhile, Bill has made up an excuse to
leave for the track, unable to resist his obsession.   The twosome meet up and bet their bundle on "Egyptian Femme."
The horse wins, and they are showered with verbal abuse by
the disconsolate Barbara.

What is important about this sequence is the way it
depicts Bill and Charlie without judging them.   In other
words, Altman is not saying that Charlie was devious in his
dealings with the young lady, but rather that he reacts according to impulse.   And, for that matter, so does Bill,

although his lack of certainty regarding the outcome of the
race contrasts sharply with Charlie's positive attitude.  In
essence, it is this contrast of behavior, as opposed to the
outcome of the actual event, which holds the scene together.
Yet despite the fact that Bill and Charlie represent two totally different personality types, they are not pitted against
one another in an effort to generate dramatic conflict.  Instead, they simply combine in a symbiotic relationship, the
real purpose of which is to provide further opportunities for
improvisational play.  One such opportunity is exemplified
in the humorous scene in which Bill and Charlie pose as
vice cops in order to oust a transvestite (Bert Remsen)
whom the girls are entertaining.  Shortly thereafter, when
Bill is indecisive about a wager, Charlie offers some advice
with the assurance that "you can bet your house on it."
Bill's comeback is, "You've been saying that for weeks--I'm
glad I'm not a property owner."  Characteristically, this exchange is also played solely for the gag, as the wager in
question never figures again in the story line.

    In the meanwhile, chance is worked into the overall
scheme of things by virtue of the fact that the blind escapism
that Charlie represents is just what Bill is apparently looking
for at this precarious moment in his life.  For although
Bill's background is left conspicuously open, Altman does include two brief scenes that offer a possible explanation for
his behavior.  The first occurs when Bill hits on an old ac-
quaintance for a loan, and the friend, Harvey, sarcastically
mentions something about Bill getting back together with his
"old lady."  In the other scene, just after his bookmaker
(played by Joseph Walsh) has put some heavy pressure on
him to pay his debts, Bill tells Susan, one of the call girls
(Gwen Welles), that he's "separated" from his wife.  These
statements serve to confirm our suspicions that Bill is essentially a displaced family man, and imply insight that
Charlie is helping to fill the emotional void caused by the
breakup of Bill's marriage.

    Suitably enough, these scenes both occur while Charlie
is mysteriously away and Bill is under severe emotional
stress.  As soon as Charlie returns, however, Bill experiences a major epiphany, in which he envisions himself becoming a big winner in Reno.  This scene is crucial since
it signals a role reversal that will be played out for the remaining half of the film.  Despite the fact that their basic
behavior patterns remain intact, it is now Bill's turn to control the action.  Charlie, on the other hand, although some-

what perplexed by this change in energy, is ready to play
along with his partner's new-found confidence.

Before they arrive in Reno, Altman inserts a curious
sequence that gives us pause to doubt the wisdom of their
impending decision.   Employing parallel-editing techniques,
Altman contrasts the two men's attempts to raise some
gambling money, intercutting shots of Bill entering a pawn-
shop and Charlie hustling some kids at basketball.   The implication that Charlie is actually better equipped to do their
gambling is also reinforced by Phyllis Shotwell's crooning
"You're an Old Smoothy" over Charlie's easy win.   On the
bus to Reno, however, Bill's sense of confidence is so over-
whelmingly intense that Charlie refuses to tamper with it.
Intuitively, Charlie has come to realize that, for the time
being at least, Bill holds the power to make or break them,
because he has absorbed his mentor's penchant for positive
thinking.

This notion of their "doubling," or "split," is carried
one step further in an ensuing scene in Reno, after Bill sits
in on a big private game.   When a professional high roller
(Amarillo Slim, playing himself) asks Charlie why he's not
playing, Charlie tells him that he is, motioning towards Bill:
"That's me, that good-looking blond fellow in the brown
coat."   And for all intents and purposes, Charlie is right,
because without his inspiration, Bill wouldn't be in the position that he's in.   The irony of the situation is that Bill is
unconsciously working up to their ultimate split by playing
on the illusion that his streak of luck will enable him to re-
gain the sense of emotional stability which he has lost.

Thus, after a quick cut to Phyllis Shotwell (whom we
have heard numerous times before, but never seen) in the
lounge, Bill gets up and announces that he "can't settle down"
with Charlie there.   Once Charlie leaves, Bill settles down
to the tune of $11,000, whereupon Charlie extends the idea
of their role reversal by advising his partner to leave.   Unlike Bill, the only "heat" that Charlie feels is his ongoing
compulsion to involve himself at any level of the action--a
compulsion that Bill repeatedly denies until the very end of
the streak.   Again, Shotwell's lyrics ("honey, you're mean
to me") comment on this interaction up until the final crap
shoot.   At this point, Bill is so sure of himself that he has
Charlie place the bets while he rolls the dice.   Then, after
an incredible run, Bill walks off with his head bowed down

while Charlie's "got the world on a string, sittin' on a
rainbow. "

        Following their "even split" ($41, 000 each), the real
climax (the real split) occurs on the heels of Bill's admission that "there was no special feeling, I just said there
was. "  Now Bill's belief that his realization has freed him
of his obsession (as expressed in the line, "Charlie, I have
to go home"), is wrenchingly undercut by Charlie's accusa-
tory reply: "Oh, yeah?  Where do you live?"  In the end,
however, Altman's concluding shot encourages us not to read
any more into these proceedings than the irrepressible Charlie does.  For after Charlie ponders them briefly, the camera zooms out as he shrugs it all off with a song, spins a
wheel of fortune, and walks away while the camera zooms
in on this recapitulative image of chance.  Then, as the
final credits appear (over the spinning wheel), Charlie can
be heard one last time, playfully "riffing" with Shotwell's
rendition of "Bye, Bye, Blackbird"--"Sounds like the story
of my life. "

### A Wedding (1978)

        Unlike California Split, which was intended to "mir-
ror" the world of gambling without making much of a statement, Nashville and A Wedding both gravitate toward social
commentary.  Recalling his original idea for A Wedding,
Altman has said that he felt that a wedding would provide
him with a fertile device "to explore the foibles of a society. "
Of course, many of Altman's films (and particularly Nashville) do this to varying degrees.  The most obvious difference is that A Wedding places its massive group of characters in a more highly controlled situation.

        After all, people behave differently when they're
        placed in formal situations.  At a wedding or a
        funeral, unless you're an out-and-out rebel, you
        follow the amenities of the culture.  You don't act
        the way you normally act; you're putting on a front.
        You're not comfortable, you're not dressed the way
        you dress at any other occasion.  So we had the
        arena for a multicast, cultural, comedy situation.11

Altman has also spoken of A Wedding as an extension of

From A Wedding

"the Nashville experiment," since the number of characters
was doubled, from twenty-four to forty-eight.   Additionally,
the action all takes place in one highly limited location, in
one day.   However, A Wedding also differs radically from
Nashville in terms of its thematic implications, intensity,
and the kind of open spaces it creates.   Because A Wedding
is in many ways less complex (and less rewarding) than
Nashville, I have chosen to discuss it first, and then to con-
clude this chapter with an analysis of Nashville.

      Due to its privileged status in terms of location and
time span, A Wedding provides us with numerous insights
into Altman's working method.   After completing a relatively
"small" film with a very complex story line (Three Women),
he embarked on a sizable project, the linear sequence of
which encompasses but one day in the lives of its characters.
Unlike Three Women (1977), A Wedding starts off like a light
comedy, but becomes progressively darker as it begins to
peel away the many façades that serve as the targets of its
satire.   Having formulated his original idea, Altman and
John Considine (the actor who portrayed Frank Butler in
Buffalo Bill) put together "an outline of character sketches,
rather than a dialogue script."   Following the protocol of a

wedding, they then blocked out a series of situations on index cards.   Next came the casting, which in this film (perhaps more than any of Altman's others) was used to round out and give shape to a large number of as yet vaguely defined characters.   At this point, two other writers were hired (Allan Nicholls and Patricia Resnick), and the cast was encouraged to seek their aid (along with Altman and Considine) in constructing their characters' background stories--a practice that had previously been employed for Nashville.

This procedure, which calls for a great amount of input on the part of the performers, is undoubtedly one of the main reasons that so many actors and actresses have the highest regard for Altman as a director.   By the same token, it also brings to light the distinction between pure improvisation and the kind of preplanned collaborative improvisation found in most of Altman's films.   While many of his performers most certainly do improvise, it is all done within a tightly controlled and predetermined structure. In this respect, Altman's overall attitude is to have his performers do what seems natural within a given situation, and if it doesn't work out, do it another way.

Another traditional Altman practice designed to create the kind of communal atmosphere reflected in many of his films is often to encourage performers to remain on location during the entire period of shooting.   For A Wedding, this amounted to eight weeks--three days in the church and the rest in the Armour mansion in Lake Bluff, Illinois.

> It [the Armour mansion] has its own place in the
> cultural history of the area....   The house is as
> you see it, except for the Italian grotto we built
> in the basement.   We chose the wardrobe, but we
> sent our cast to some wedding people we'd hired
> as consultants.   And they told us the protocol;
> they did the flowers, they dressed the church;
> they chose the cake; they picked the menu; they
> put the tent up; they selected the presents.   We
> let the people who would actually stage a wedding
> for one of those rich families stage our wedding. [12]

As in California Split, sound goes hand in hand with the use of these naturalistic details.   During much of the shooting, as many as fourteen people were miked, a feat that was accomplished by the simultaneous operation of two eight-track units.

   A Wedding relies upon two central thematic devices
to make the majority of its satirical points.   The first entails the contrast of the Southern nouveau-riche family of the
bride with the groom's more traditionally established Mid-
western family.   The second has to do with the fact that
nearly every character is involved to one degree or another
with some kind of personal secret.   On one level then, the
film's open spaces (such as they are) are bound up with the
audience's attempts to sort out this complex series of interrelationships and penetrate the various façades set up by each
of the characters.   But, as is often the case with Altman's
films, there is also another level (which might be called a
"secret agenda"), which refers to both American society at
large and to the filmmaking process.   Of course, as we have
already seen (cf. M*A*S*H), the mere existence of this other
level in no way ensures its success.   However, our awareness of how it operates in A Wedding is crucial to our understanding of Altman's overall narrative strategy.

   Although A Wedding is filled with a wide variety of
visual symbols and metaphors, there are four shots in particular that, considered as a unit, come the closest to revealing what this secret agenda is all about.   These four
shots are all reverse zooms accompanied by brass fanfares.
Two of the four serve as the film's opening and closing
shots, while the remaining two come at strategic points
relatively early in the action.   The first shot entails an establishing zoom-out from the church altar, which, together
with the brass section's ponderous fanfare, imbues the first
few moments of A Wedding with a grandly reverential tone.
However, this tone (and the shot) is swiftly undercut in a
manner that virtually ensures that it will never again be recaptured.   This occurs when our attention is diverted to a
rustling in the wings marked by snatches of overlapping dialogue.   A scrambling figure (Lauren Hutton) annoyingly asks,
"Where do you want me to sit?," and an unidentified voice
tells her to sit on her foot.   This brief exchange, which is
antithetical to the establishing tone, leads to a subtly stated
synthesis when the camera proceeds to reveal that the speak-
ers are members of a small film crew.   The emerging dialectic can be rephrased as follows:   thesis (reverence) plus
antithesis (irreverence) equals synthesis (the filmmaking
process).

   The next two reverse zooms are used to bridge the
action between the wedding ceremony and the reception prep-
arations.   Reminiscent of the P. A. transition in M*A*S*H,
both of these shots serve the self-reflexive function of calling

attention to the film's shaping intelligence, and also comment on the shots that precede them.   The second of these
reverse zooms (from the façade of the mansion) comes just
after Muffin (Amy Stryker) exposes her braces while acknowl-
edging her wedding vows.   The third follows the sequence in
which the bishop (John Cromwell) fumbles around for the
rings.   The film's final shot (which also zooms out from the
side of the mansion) acts as a coda that sums up all that has
preceded it.   Taken as a unit, then, because these four shots
all originate from façades, they can be seen as a master
metaphor (or elaborate visual puns) that enables Altman to
orient our reactions.   In other words, they exemplify a
strategy by which Altman can simultaneously distance us
from the action and repeatedly express his overview that
the very substance of A Wedding is based on a façade that
the filmmaking process is uniquely empowered to reveal.

A Wedding can also be characterized by the tension
that it attempts to generate by counterposing naturalistic and
non-naturalistic techniques.   Along with the self-delusions
manifested by his characters, this tension is at the core of
Altman's bisociative narrative structures.   In my analysis of
M*A*S*H, it was discussed in terms of illusionist versus
"overt" devices.   It also figures in California Split in the
way that notions of play are integrated into various levels of
the text.   Similarly, A Wedding uses a host of overt devices
(in addition to the abovementioned master-metaphor) that jar
the viewer's consciousness.   This is the essence of Altman's
modernist strategy:   to inundate the spectator with bisociative
themes and structures that serve as a catalyst for open-ended
audience interactions.

The most prominent of these devices involves Altman's
(self-reflexive) use of filmic references.   These come in four
distinct varieties, all of which add a measure of bisociative
complexity to the text.   The first type includes overt verbal
references (to films) made by the characters.   Similar in
impact to the plethora of filmic references found in both
Truffaut's and Godard's early films, many of these originate
with Hughie (Dennis Cristopher), Muffin's kid brother.   For
example, when the groom, Dino Corelli (Desi Arnaz, Jr.),
and his friends indulge in some homosexually oriented humor
("He's interested in everybody's fly"), Hughie interjects a
note of bisociative humor into the proceedings with his comment, "Oh, The Fly.   That was a great picture."   Similarly, while the boys try to figure out a way to put a frog into
the wedding couple's bed, Hughie asks them if they have ever

heard of a movie called Frogs.   This technique crops up in
at least two other instances.   The first involves Carol Bur-
nett's unappreciated--by the straitlaced aunt of the groom,
Antoinette Goddard (Dina Merrill)--revelation that she once
"had the same experience as that girl in Carrie. "   The other
instance occurs when Lauren Hutton mistakenly addresses
Louis Corelli (Vittorio Gassman), the father of the groom,
as Mr. Corleone (cf. The Godfather).   This last example is
a bit more complex than the others because Corelli's mysterious background (he is rumored to have Mafia connections)
is one of A Wedding's major secrets.

Another type of reference employs scenes that recall
other films.   Among these, the most obvious include Altman's depiction of what is presumed to be the bride's and
groom's accidental death (cf. the car wreck in Godard's
Contempt), and the ensemble's singing of "Heavenly Sunlight"
in the darkened cellar (cf. "When the Lights Go On Again"
in M*A*S*H).   A third type involves the previously mentioned
film crew, who are constantly on the lookout for revealing
"actualities. "   An interesting example of this occurs when
Altman films them filming Buffy (Mia Farrow), Muffin's
sister, who poses topless in front of a similar portrait (a
wedding gift painted by "a very important socialist-minded
young artist") of Muffin.

Finally, there are the traditional Altmanesque signatures or stamps (e. g., overlapping dialogue, moving camera,
zooms, the use of mirrors and reflecting surfaces), all of
which are self-reflexive in the sense that they call attention
to themselves and distance us from the action, even if we
are not intimately familiar with the rest of Altman's work.
Besides the use of self-reflexive narrative strategies, the
group of films here under consideration (M*A*S*H, California Split, Nashville, and A Wedding) all rely on parallel-
editing techniques, which counteract the sense of realism
fostered by Altman's structural use of naturalistic detail.
They do this by fragmenting the flow of their linear sequences.   This technique also shifts the burden of the riddle to the spectator.   But once again, we are faced with
the question of the resultant payoff.   In A Wedding, the
most obvious, and perhaps the only, answer is humor.

Thus, following the first sequence, the opening credits appear over a brief scene that strains to reinforce the
film's comic climate.   As she walks down the aisle, we
notice that the bride has a big spot on her dress that, some-

one comments, "looks like a fly; looks like someone crushed
a fly on her dress." Dutifully, Hutton and her film crew
take all this in (end credits). Then, as the spoken part of
the service begins (accompanied by cutaways to various as-
yet-unidentified participants), the bishop has to be told the
bride's and groom's names as a prelude to Muffin's "un-
veiling." This baring of her braces is a comic flourish
that Altman has attempted to maximize by showing Muffin
with her mouth tightly closed in all of her previous shots.

After the second reverse zoom, the introduction of
Nettie Sloan (Lillian Gish) and her nurse provides Altman
with an opportunity to lay the groundwork for A Wedding's
most recurrent motif. Interestingly enough, it is Gish, the
matriarchal head of the groom's family, and the source of
many of their secrets, who uncovers the first secret in the
film. Starting off on a minor key, this initial revelation,
which involves the nurse's smoking, is soon followed by
more complex matters, as Gish confers with Randolph
(Cedric Scott), the Sloans' black servant. This complexity
is presaged by the tender manner (they hold hands) in which
Gish instructs Randolph to be on his best behavior ("no conversations with my daughter in front of the guests"). Moments later, in what Altman has referred to as "the death
of a silent screen star," Gish passes away in front of her
nurse and the wedding coordinator (Geraldine Chaplin).

Very shortly, this inauspicious turn of events will
serve as a catalyst for a whole other series of secrets, but
for the present our attention is diverted to Chaplin's typically farcical reaction. After pausing for a moment in a state
of stunned disbelief, she suddenly remembers something
about the wedding cake and frantically exits the room. Thus,
despite her previous admonition that "this isn't a circus, it's
a wedding," Chaplin is portrayed as a rather ludicrous ringmaster, whose function it is to choreograph and announce the
various "acts" of the wedding. Of course, the real prime
mover of A Wedding is none other than Altman himself, a
fact that is reaffirmed as the wedding procession arrives at
the mansion. This is accomplished by transforming one of
the day's more minor events into a bravura audiovisual
"happening." As the cars approach the house (accompanied
by the fanfare), the camera zooms out to reveal a gift-
wrapped Mercedes parked in the center of a circular drive.
Rather than cutting away from this scene to some interior
action (as the film's pacing up to this point has conditioned
us to expect), Altman follows this shot with a high-angled

long take in which the other cars form a perfect circle
around the Mercedes.   During this action the soundtrack has
switched to Italian strings, but as the cars are unloaded, it
begins to pick up various bits of barely distinguishable dialogue.

Like M*A*S*H, California Split, and Nashville, A
Wedding runs the gamut of comic styles, from the most subtle to the most broad.   Thus, while the scene in the circular drive more closely approximates the former, Carol Bur-
nett's portrayal of Tulip Brenner, the nouveau-riche mother
of the bride, is both suitably and consistently in line with
the latter of these styles.   For example, when we first
meet Tulip, she is asking Louis Corelli what kind of car it
is that everyone is making such a fuss over.   When he
proudly tells her it's a "Merchedis," she mimics his pro-
nunciation and adds, "Now I speak Italian."   Later--in addition to her pivotal scenes with Mackenzie (Mac) Goddard
(Pat McCormick)--she is also guilty of committing several
humorous faux pas (one of which involves the Carrie reference) that offend members of the Corelli/Sloan family.

Once they have returned from the church, Altman
divides the wedding party into several groups the better to
acquaint us with the participants.   These groupings also
draw on various comic styles, ranging from the Brenner
women's farcical search for a toilet in an enormous mirrored bathroom, to the understated little sojourn by Mac,
Snooks (Paul Dooley, the father of the bride), and Corelli
to Louis's subterranean "kingdom," an "exact replica" of
his "favorite cafe in Rome."   It is at this point that Altman
thrusts an anomolous character (Buffy) into the fray in a
manner calculated to break up the flow of his linear sequence.   That is, after Muffin thanks her silent sister for
being her maid of honor, Buffy looks at herself in a mirror, and splashes water on her reflection while the camera
zooms in.   Typically, Altman uses both the zoom and a reflecting surface, as well as Buffy's silence, to provoke our
own reflections as to the possible significance of this discordant action.

Building layer upon layer, such anomalies as the
Mia Farrow character represents are blended with the motifs of guarded secrets and filmmaking references to underscore the discrepancy between appearance and reality, a
discrepancy that serves as A Wedding's thematic center.
Among these recurrent motifs, the wide variety of secrets

that hold the action together are undoubtedly the most important, for secrets, like façades, are the means by which
Altman's characters delude themselves, as well as others.
Accordingly, Altman's own secret agenda can be seen to entail the revelation that what prevents his characters from
achieving the sense of unity symbolized by the wedding ritual
is the divisive nature of their secret delusions.

The problem with this strategy, however, is that because Altman's characters are such obvious vehicles for his
complex machinations, this deeper level is denied the structural machinery necessary for it to surface.   In other words,
the feeling that these characters were brought into existence
solely for the purpose of this event strips A Wedding of its
dialectical potential.   Although the film may succeed as a
humorous exploration of "the foibles of a society," the limited depth of its characters and situations actually provokes
a sense of closure that comes perilously close to defeating
this very purpose.   The result is a pastiche of consistently
comic vignettes that fail to sustain more than a modicum of
reflection.

The sequences that focus on Tulip's and Mac's infatu-
ation put many of these issues into a clearer perspective.
Handled in a broad comic style, this subplot plays upon the
illusion/reality dichotomy in a manner that is far from ambiguous.   That is, much of its humor is derived from the
fact that the couple's secret romance is such an obvious
sham.   At the same time, Altman provides us with a comic
twist by revealing the great lengths that the pair go to in
order to ensure the secrecy of their blatantly self-deluded
relationship.   The problem, again, is that Altman simply
uses this situation as a pretext to run through a litany of
comic gags that merely reiterate what we already know.
Thus, after Tulip rejects Mac's initial advances, Altman
cuts to a subsequent scene in which Tulip looks at herself
in a mirror while "Love Is Lovelier the Second Time
Around" plays on the soundtrack.   In this way, Altman
makes it quite clear that what Tulip is actually falling for
is the clichéd illusion of romance.

The couple's greenhouse tryst enlarges upon these
themes, as the two "lovers" run toward each other in a
wide-angled shot that is climaxed by their inevitable crash.
Amidst these clichés (she says they "can't go on meeting
like this," etc.), Altman does manage to salvage the scene
by interjecting a humorous bit that transcends its predicta-

bility up to this point.  This occurs when a group of kids
interrupts their meeting, prompting Tulip to make believe
that she's out there looking for an earring.  She offers a
quarter's reward to anyone who can find it, to which Mac
chimes in, "Make that a hundred dollars!"

Mac's wife, Toni, is another character fraught with
self-delusions.  As Gish's eldest daughter, she takes it upon
herself to act as the nominal head of the family in her mother's absence.  Her obsession with this role is well noted by
many of the other members of the family, who keep Gish's
death a secret in order to indulge Toni's fantasies.  The
most prominent of these characters is her sister Grace,
whose affair with Randolph has been sanctioned by Gish,
who's afraid that Toni "will just die if she finds out that I
knew about it first."  And so it is that events that might
conceivably bring people together (like a wedding) are subverted by secrets that invariably keep them apart.

Another example of this involves Buffy's secret (that
she's been impregnated by Dino), which both separates her
from Muffin and eventually threatens the culmination of the
wedding itself.  Louis Corelli's secret (his shady background)
also has a similar effect.  In fact, he has been putting up a
front for so long that, by his own admission, he "can't even
remember his real name."  The irony of this situation is
that his secret has such a grip on his psyche that he fails
to realize that Gish's death has freed him of his obligations.
Consequently, he flails away at his brother, oblivious to the
fact that his long-standing agreement with Gish (that he loses
everything if a member of his family sets foot in their house)
is no longer in effect.  However, because the complexities of
this situation fail to engage us beyond the superficial level of
concealed information, these ambiguous narrative structures
only result in gratuitous confusion.

Amidst all these other secrets, Altman conjures up
one of his own, which is used to provoke a final confrontation between the two families.  After the Brenners leave the
mansion, he cuts to an ambulance and the camera begins to
move in on the burning Mercedes, which has jack-knifed
under a truck (cf. Contempt).  After another zoom-in on the
wreckage, the Brenners, who, along with most of the audience, believe that Dino and Muffin are dead, decide to turn
back and inform the Corellis.  When they arrive, everybody's
partying, including Buffy, who's been inexplicably left behind.
Then, after Hughie lowers the boom by revealing what they

have just witnessed, the party explodes into a series of re-
criminations.   Centering mainly on the two families' differences rather than their mutual loss, these petty bickerings
reach a climax of sorts when Toni calls Snooks "a truck
driver" and he replies that he made over five million dollars in the last year alone.

        These perfunctory jibes at American class conscious-
ness are mercifully curtailed a few moments later when
Muffin, and then Dino, appear at the top of the stairs.   Realizing it was Briggs (Gavin O'Herlihy) who was driving the
car, everyone rejoices, with the exception of Buffy, who
covers her ears to block out the din.   In the end, Altman
focuses on a minor character (Leslie Rogers) in a manner
that attempts to sum up his bisociative themes and structure.
After tilting down to a shot of Rogers and Geraldine Chaplin,
the latter comments that weddings are "so lovely, but when
they're over it's always so sad. "   This is followed by the
final reverse zoom, over which Rogers adds that her own
wedding was also beautiful, "but you're right, when it's over
it gets real sad. "   The irony of this concluding exchange is
manifold, for, in addition to the event that we have just witnessed having been anything but "beautiful, " Chaplin has been
revealed to be a lesbian and the Rogers' marriage has been
exposed as yet another sham.   Moreover, this last revelation is so casually brought to light (we get a brief glimpse
of Rogers's husband making love to a friend of the bride's
in the bushes) that the viewer can only wonder if Rogers's
statement implies a realization of her self-delusions, or
whether she is merely echoing Altman's self-reflexive sentiments on what it feels like to be finished with his film.

Nashville (1975)

        Although Nashville and A Wedding share many struc-
tural similarities, the former is a much more ambitious attempt to integrate bisociative themes and structures.   Pin-
pointing one of the major differences between these two films,
screenwriter Joan Tewkesbury has said that "the whole piece
[Nashville] was about people who were trying to do the best
job they could with the equipment they had in this dumb kind
of social structure. "[13]   In other words, whereas A Wedding
actually trivializes "the foibles of a society" through the
humorous obfuscation of their real origin, Nashville stead-

From Nashville

fastly avoids this sense of closure by making the social system an integral part of the film's overall structure.

     Nashville thrives on internal contradictions.   Accord-
ingly, Altman's "vision" bears a dialectical relationship to
the "product" that he and his collaborators have attempted
to create.   In Nashville, this vision centers on the "other-
directed" tendencies of American society, what Tewkesbury
refers to as "this dumb kind of social structure."   It is
this social structure that is the real villain of the piece.
Here, openness has become a tyranny and the community a
mirage.   But Nashville refutes its own thesis.   It is both
open and synergetic.   This synthesis resides in the spectator's attempts to resolve its inherent contraditions.   Once
we understand the dual nature of this vision, a transformation occurs because, according to dialectical process, internal contradiction breeds development.   This is what the
synergistic response is all about; internal contradictions
within the work are structured in such a way that their interrogation entails a corresponding interrogation of the
viewer's own codes and contradictions.

     The first step in this process involves the ways in
which Altman bombards the viewer with bisociative experience

capable of jarring the spectator's consciousness.  In Nashville, the fact that this process is initiated from the very
beginning is particularly significant.   Even before the film's
first live-action image appears, Nashville sets its dialectical
structure in motion.   It accomplishes this by opening with an
ironically raucous advertisement for itself which attempts to
"sell" Nashville to the audience.   In effect, this introduction
functions as a microcosm of the entire film by confronting
the viewer with such pivotal dichotomies as production/con-
sumption and illusionism/self-reflexivity, right off the bat.

On the audiovisual level, this bisociative assault is
unleashed through the efforts of an unseen announcer who
barks out a stream of superlatives as he introduces the
film's twenty-four "stars," many of whom the audience probably never heard of.   Simultaneously, the "stars'" faces appear on the screen, interspersed with the titles of the film's
"hit songs" and the title of the film itself--which is repeatedly flashed across the wide screen.   As this barrage dies
down, a garage (live-action) opens, and a red-white-and-blue
van, replete with political posters for one Hal Philip Walker,
emerges.   Evidently, according to the posters, Walker is
the presidential candidate for the Replacement Party.   We
hear his taped speech as the van moves down Middle American streets littered with signs and symbols of the society.

Our recognition of the fact that this "selling of a
president" very closely parallels the film's selling of itself
may not be as obvious upon first viewing as it is in retrospect.   For Altman's strategy of bombardment provides the
spectator with such an overload of bisociative stimuli that he
is constantly forced to readjust his perceptions.   Moreover,
new ingredients are continually being blended in a manner
that shatters initial impressions by the dual process of offering up one level of experience that can only be interpreted in
retrospect, while simultaneously bombarding the viewer with
another level that elicits an immediate response.

The introduction of Haven Hamilton (Henry Gibson)
provides us with a rich example of the way this process
works.   Cutting from the Walker van to the interior of a recording studio, we are once more confronted by a dazzling
array of bisociative structures.   Because the camera is moving and there is not as yet any specific focal point for the
viewer's gaze, the most prominent of these structures has to
do with the soundtrack.   For the same reason, in visual
terms, suspense is generated by the camera's initial avoid-

ance of the source of the sound.  Its movement, which we
assume is toward that source, also creates a sense of kines-
thesia.  Still, it is the song on the soundtrack, "200 Years,"
and its lyrics that are most likely to capture our attention.
In brief, the song is a rather jingoistic celebration of American history whose meaning is well summarized by the often
repeated refrain, "O, we must be doin' somethin' right to
last 200 years."

Once the singer is identified as Henry Gibson, another
range of bisociative associations comes into play.  Henry
Gibson, that Laugh-In regular, playing a country singer (Haven Hamilton)?  Such a questioning response is indeed a
probable one in view of the fact that Altman has not really
keyed us into his intentions.  Thus, when Henry/Haven
stops the number midway through in order to complain about
the annoying presence of one of the many spectators (looking
in through the glass separation), we get our first indication
that Henry may actually be playing it straight.  Then, when
he interrupts the song once again to complain about the
piano player, Frog (Richard Baskin), we begin to realize
that whether this is satire or not, Gibson certainly takes
himself seriously.  Additionally, his subsequent comments
that the long-haired Frog "ought to get a haircut" and that
he doesn't "belong in Nashville," begin to round out his
present redneck persona.

At the same time, in thematic terms, the openness
of this sequence, or our inability to pin it down any further,
leads us back to a consideration of the implications of Gibson's lyrics, and the possible object, if any, of Altman's
satire.  Because we don't know any more than we do either
about Gibson (we don't even know that he's Haven Hamilton
yet) or Nashville, we will have to wait before we can sur-
mise very much more.  In the meanwhile, though, a chain
of interlinking associations has been started which may eventually lead us to an interrogation of our own codes.  Maybe
not.  In any event, the open-ended complexity of the presen-
tation, which also includes cuts to another bisociative scene,
ensures that the seeds will be planted for such an eventuality.

The other related scene, which is motivated by Gibson's initial annoyance, commences when the singer's son,
Bud Hamilton (David Peel), takes the nosey offender, Opal
(Geraldine Chaplin), to an adjoining studio.  Here, Lily Tomlin, another Laugh-In regular, is singing lead in an otherwise all-black gospel session.  Once again, bisociative associations abound.  The real achievement of this entire

sequence is that it can support so many contradictory interpretations.   These may range from the supposition that it
represents a slur on Nashville--or, by extension, a condem-
nation of Middle America as a whole--to the feeling that it
is merely a light parody of Nashville, or a parody of paro-
dies.   Still, other critics have suggested that the film is
simply Hollywood's (or Altman's) vision of what Nashville is
actually like.

      In any case, it is only in retrospect that we realize
that Altman's self-reflexive show-business allusions are integrated into the total sociopolitical structure of the film, and
that this controls their meaning.   It is this realization that
transforms Altman's "personal" vision (the "Hollywood" vision of Nashville or American life) into a potentially synergistic experience.   This is what differentiates Nashville from
many of Altman's other films (including M*A*S*H, California
Split and A Wedding)--the fact that this social dimension has
become an integral part of the structure.   On one level,
this social dimension revolves around an invisible center
(Hal Philip Walker, whom we never see), which is one reason why the film maintains a fundamental sense of openness
characteristic of Altman's modernism.   On another level,
though, this open or invisible center is analogous to the
American dilemma as Altman and his collaborators seem to
see it.   That is, the inability of our society to attain a
meaningful sense of community because of external or "other-
directed" motivations.   This is graphically illustrated by the
way that characters are brought together by chance (in the
freeway accident, at the airport, Parthenon, etc. ), but are
separated by choices that reflect their conflicting visions in
terms of external motivations, attitudes, and goals.

      After Barbara Jean (Ronee Blakley) collapses at the
airport, Altman uses the massive freeway tie-up as a humorous metaphor for our society's state of confusion.   Beginning with a shot of the omnipresent tricycle man (Jeff Gold-
blum), streams of traffic pour out of the airport parking lot,
literally devour a mechanical gate, only to be left motion-
less along a long expanse of freeway, following a chain-
reaction collision.   However, Opal's comment that "it's
America" is only a half-truth in the present instance, for
Altman uses the situation to bring his broad band of characters together in a way that would not have been possible
otherwise.   Then, as the tricycle man leaves the fray, a
strategic cut to the Walker van as it passes by Barbara
Jean's hospital window leads into a tracking shot inside a
local bluegrass club.

The ensuing sequence provides a sharp contrast to the accident by intercutting scenes between the bluegrass club and Deemen's Den, a local bar where amateur acts audition for the public.   In this case, the characters are separated by choices that point toward their overall social status, while the freeway has proved to be the great equalizer.   Even more indicative of the way that these Nashville denizens divide their allegiances is a subsequent sequence that cuts from a zoom-in to a smug close-up of one of Tom's (Keith Carradine) many sexual flings to a series of shots representing various places of worship.   Beginning with a small Catholic service, Altman cuts to a more ornate Baptist church attended by many of Nashville's most solid citizens.   The most promi-nent of these is Del Reese (Ned Beatty) and his children, and Haven Hamilton, who is singing in the choir.   The next cut is to a black Baptist church attended by Beatty's wife (Lily Tomlin) and Tommy Brown (Timmy Brown), among others.   This series of shots then culminates with a cut to Barbara Jean in the hospital chapel before the camera pulls back to reveal various other characters who are attending the hospital service for one reason or another.

One of Nashville's main bisociative themes plays upon discrepancies between appearance and reality in relationship to the "open society" hinted at by the film's many Bicenten-nial motifs.   However, unlike A Wedding, in which most of the characters never rise above their narrow stereotypes, Nashville views its characters in a lot more depth.   Thus, although most of the film's personages are satirized to vary-ing degrees, they are also treated with a certain amount of respect as befits those who, to paraphrase Tewkesbury, try to do the best they can within this crazy social structure. Put another way, in terms of Altman's typical auteurist structure, they are invariably lauded for their efforts to "survive."   This, in essence, accounts for the double-edged meaning in Haven Hamilton's "We must be doin' somethin' right to last 200 years."   For, although Hamilton is unques-tionably representative of the shrewd realist who crops up in so many of Altman's works, the fact that he is not in con-flict with the "dreamers" renders him a more indirect object of Altman's satire.   The main target, again, is the social system itself.

Unlike such a film as Brewster McCloud, which dissi-pates its sense of social resonance by contrasting an impos-sible dream with the harsh reality of the system, Nashville achieves resonance by integrating "dream-come-true" figures like Haven Hamilton with impossible dreamers, represented

here by Albuquerque (Barbara Harris) and Sueleen Gay (Gwen
Welles).   This makes the text as a microcosm appear to be
truly open (cf. "the open society") in the sense that anything
can happen (a little boy can grow up to be the President,
Haven Hamilton/Henry Gibson can become a "star").   On a
deeper level, this same kind of open-endedness (as portrayed
in the film's "It don't worry me" conclusion) reveals an ultimate lack of meaning or distortion of same, which is brought
about by the social system.   This new meaning, or the dialectical revelation of this deeper meaning, is what permeates
the invisible core of the narrative and gives it resonance.

The above is one of the many reasons why it is so
hard to pin down Altman's themes.   Once again, the director's narrative strategy works at cross-purposes to the for-
mulation of "right" or one-dimensional answers.   Thus, when
Hamilton's mistress, Lady Pear (Barbara Baxley), tells a
political organizer, John Triplette (Michael Murphy), that the
only time she ever "went hog wild was over the Kennedy
boys," our reactions are left cooperatively open, because
Altman's wry sense of distance substitutes the modern artist's palette for the preacher's pulpit.   In other words, aside
from the retrospective ramifications of her assassination references, it is the nuances of her tone and delivery that engage us, rather than the foreshadowing of which we can not
as yet be aware.

Sueleen Gay is an entirely different type of character
who, along with Albuquerque, comes closest to embodying
Nashville's pervasive sense of openness gone beserk.   Sold
on the idea of becoming a sexier version of Barbara Jean,
Sueleen first appears in the film singing in the cafe where
she works as a waitress.   Curiously enough, it is during
this scene that Ned Beatty (who also appears for the first
time in this scene) reacts to something that may or may not
be Sueleen's song.   In any event, a typically oblique link is
established between these two characters early on, as is the
fact that Sueleen can't sing worth a damn.   However, when
she next appears, auditioning at Deemen's Den, the club's
proprietor figures that she would be just about right for the
promotional smoker being organized by Beatty and Murphy.
Still convinced of her dream, Sueleen misinterprets this action as a confirmation of her talent.

What is most remarkable about Altman's treatment of
Sueleen is the amount of sympathy that he elicits for this ostensible object of ridicule.   Initially, this feeling resides in

the fact that none of the other characters are willing to undercut her childlike illusions.   Additionally, Altman inserts
two brief scenes of Sueleen practicing in front of her mirror,  scenes that add a measure of complexity to this portrait of one of humanity's most vulnerable members.    This
is accomplished by having Sueleen pad her bra and continually primp, in what comes off as a seemingly subconscious
effort to compensate for her lack of talent.

The smoker itself is undoubtedly one of the highlights
of the film.    Lowered from the rafters via a movable stage,
Welles's physical presence is powerful enough to sustain her
middle-aged audience at first,  in spite of her almost ludicrous inability to carry a tune.    Also, the central irony of
the situation is derived from the fact that, although it has
never been overtly mentioned, Welles is still the only one
who fails to realize what is actually required of her.    This
lack of recognition is compounded when, midway through her
first number, Triplette appears to be the only character who
seems to be aware of her deficiencies.    Thus, when her audience finally reaches its inevitable state of restlessness,
Sueleen has nary a clue as to what is actually going on.

Finally,  Triplette and Reese are forced to intercede
as her audience's raucousness has virtually paralyzed the
would-be young star.    Afraid that their fund-raising effort
(for Hal Philip Walker) is about to go down the drain, Triplette attempts to salvage the situation by offering Welles the
"impossible" opportunity to perform at the Parthenon with
Barbara Jean, if she will just fulfill her present obligation.
Faced with this dilemma, Welles opts to disrobe to the overwhelming approval of the crowd, which remains impervious
to her futile attempts to hold back her tears.    After taking
her home, Beatty's furtive attempt to seduce her is interrupted by the arrival of Wade (Robert Doqui), who tells his
friend (their exact relationship is never made clear) that
she can't sing.    But even he can't dissuade her.    After all,
she's just been offered the ultimate chance--to appear on the
same bill with Barbara Jean.

In addition to such "realists" and "dreamers" as Haven Hamilton and Sueleen Gay, Nashville is also peopled by
a more balanced set of characters who help it to achieve a
sense of verisimilitude.    Among these, the improbable twosome of Lily Tomlin and Ned Beatty are the most noteworthy.
Because these two individuals--who seem to have almost
nothing in common--have managed to sustain what is probably

the most stable relationship in Nashville, they provide us
with a striking illustration of Altman's sense of coherent
contradiction.   The Reeses' first scene together is particularly revealing of the way Altman uses the nuances of his
characters' behavior to communicate a plethora of meaning.
Thus, the couple's understated reactions to their deaf son's
seemingly innocuous "goldfish" story tells us a great deal
about Del and Linnea (the Tomlin character's name).   What
is most notable here is the impression of spontaneous improvisation which Beatty and Tomlin lend to the scene.   For
example, the Beatty character rushes his son into his story
and then sits back, obviously absorbed in his own thoughts,
while Tomlin's every mannerism speaks of sincere concern.
Altman handles all this in revealing close-ups that tend to
separate the characters, but, at the same time, he provides
us with constant reminders that the Reeses are a viable
family unit.   These two characters are also rounded out in
other ways.   Beatty's apparent one-dimensionality is balanced
out by the basic humanity of his dogged "trying to do the best
he can" attitude, while Tomlin's "too good to be true" excesses are undercut on more than one occasion.

At the other end of the spectrum are the "outsiders"
who have come to Nashville to further their own purposes.
Opal and John Triplette are the most conspicuous of these,
along with such peripheral characters as Kenny, L. A. Joan
(Shelley Duvall), and the tricycle man.   Because Opal--who
claims to be making a documentary for the BBC but may,
in fact, be just another star-gazing freak--embodies the
worst aspects of Altman's "smart-ass and cutie-pie" tendencies, such critics as Robin Wood have deemed her responsible for Nashville's central failure.   However, Wood's argument that, as outside interviewer, she is the only character
in the film with the distance that might make possible an
understanding of the moral and emotional confusion in which
everyone else is trapped is unsound.   The problem with it
is that Opal, quite apart from her admitted excesses, is no
more of an outsider in the broad sense of the word than are
any of Nashville's other characters.   As a product of the
same social system that formed the personalities of the other
characters, Opal could not be played as anything other than
yet another variation without destroying Altman's overriding
structural patterns.   Moreover, such an attempt would only
detract from the implied message that the moral and emotional confusion that pervades Nashville is the inevitable result of the social system that Altman is depicting.

John Triplette is another ostensible outsider whose

actions make it clear that Nashville embraces more than a
small conclave in the American South.   Hal Philip Walker's
political organizer, the smooth-talking Triplette will say or
do anything to further his boss's chances.   At the same
time, Triplette is one of the few characters who does
have enough sense of distance from the Nashville scene to
see through its surface glitter.   However, aside from the
relatively inconsequential matters of personal taste (i. e.,
he puts down country music, Connie White's dress, etc.),
Triplette functions in a state of moral and emotional confusion that is virtually identical to that of the "yokels" he so
graciously condescends to.

        In a similar vein, the non-country singers (Tom,
Bill, and Mary) are not really outsiders because they have
come to Nashville to push their own careers.   For these
very same reasons, Triplette has an easy time convincing
them to perform at the Parthenon benefit for Hal Philip
Walker, despite the fact that they're "registered Democrats."
Because of their skin color, the two blacks in the film
(Robert Doqui and Timothy Brown) are representative of the
ways in which another type of potential outsider is assimilated into the Nashville scene.   Accordingly, Brown's status
as Nashville's token black star is pointed out very early
during the scene at the Exit/In, in which the drunken Doqui
assails him as "the whitest nigger I've ever seen."

        Because she is both the most revered and visibly un-
stable character in Nashville, Barbara Jean functions as a
sort of fulcrum for Altman's bisociative themes.   Idealized
in part through the efforts of her husband/manager, Barnett
(Allen Garfield), Barbara Jean seems to exist in some ethe-
real limbo that transcends the more mundane categories of
realists and dreamers.   High-strung and fantasy-prone,
Barbara Jean's main problem is that, as a victim of success, she has hardly any control at all over her own dreams
and wishes.   Consequently, her schizophrenic breakdowns
are emblematic of the communal malaise (the lack of integration) that has made her what she is.   To a great extent,
this also explains why it is Barbara Jean (and not Hal Philip
Walker) who becomes the climactic target of the young assassin's bullet.

        Many of the best-played scenes in Nashville revolve
around the relationships between paradoxically complementary
couples.   In addition to the Reeses' scene mentioned above,
the confrontation between Barbara Jean and Barnett, which

transpires during the Grand Ole Opry show, displays Altman's skillful use of his performers in a most intriguing
manner.   Unable to perform at the Opry due to her recent
collapse, Barbara Jean is getting restless in her hospital
bed, while Barnett listens to the show on the radio.   Jeal-
ous of her substitute, Connie White (Karen Black), who's
just come on, Barbara Jean asks Barnett to turn the radio
off, which causes Barnett to leap into a revealing tirade.
Screaming that he doesn't tell her how to sing, Barnett follows this up with the exquisitely ironic line, "Don't tell me
how to run your life; I've been doing pretty good at it."
This is followed by some brilliant improvisation (involving
his "hobnobbing"), after which Barnett commands her not to
"go nutsy on me."   Reduced to a childlike state by this
manipulative realist, Barbara Jean is then forced into a
litany of subservience that cruelly recalls the "three questions" that were used to such a different effect in George
Cukor's Pat and Mike.

Given the expansiveness of Nashville's 159 minutes
(reduced from over eight hours of original footage), it is
not hard to see why Robin Wood labeled it "the supreme example of the spiritual-intellectual disaster movie, with that
multi-plot, multi-character structure essential to the genre."
But, whereas this oppressive social milieu makes survival
next to impossible for such potentially "inner-directed" characters as Barbara Jean, and taints its achievement for all
of the others, Nashville itself averts disaster through its
own unique brand of openness.   Again, this is due, in part,
to the incredible scope of Altman's bisociative structure,
whose radiation from the invisible core, represented by the
Walker campaign, self-reflexively proclaims Nashville's
most meaningful intimations of what survival entails.

Among the film's many subplots, Walker's political
campaign, this "selling of the president," involves the greatest number of major characters.   Another that deals with the
disintegration of traditional institutions (the family), revolves
around Keenan Wynn's motley nuclear unit, which includes
L. A. Joan, Pfc. Glenn Kelly, and Kenny Fraiser, the young
assassin.   Besides those scenes already mentioned, interper-
sonal relationships (especially those involving "love") are depicted as being virtually unobtainable in the series of one-
night stands that Keith Carradine, as Tom, drags himself
through.   Carradine's "I'm Easy" number, performed at the
Exit/In, provides us with a particularly vivid example of the
way that Altman links his musical structures to other bisoci-

ative elements of the narrative.   Combining various aspects
of recurrent Nashville motifs having to do with professional
and sexual rivalries with the double-edged lyrics of Carradine's song (music and lyrics by Carradine), Altman literally forces his audience to cooperate with this deflation of his
characters' self-illusions.

Rather than taking the easy way out--which would be
to leave it unclear as to which of the four women present
(L. A. Joan, Opal, Mary, or Linnea) Carradine is singing
to--Altman actually complicates the situation by subtly
zooming in on Linnea.   It soon becomes apparent that the
riddle that Altman is posing transcends the question of petty
jealousies by invoking the more weighty conundrum of the
failure of love in general.   In other words, this scene serves
to generate a sense of emotional tension that Tom and Linnea's subsequent rendezvous cannot possibly sustain.   Although their meeting is punctuated by moments of genuine
tenderness, in sharp contrast to Tom's other affairs, it ends
just as shabbily.

The final paradox is that despite its often overwhelming intimations of pessimism, Nashville is a positively motivated artwork whose intricate themes and structures evince
a strong sense of faith in humanity as a whole.   Moreover,
it is a sense of faith that the viewing public will respond to
its nonconventionality in a synergetic manner.   At the same
time, we should not lose sight of the fact that the formal
risks that Altman has taken are part and parcel of this positive experience.   Thus, on the formal level of aesthetics,
Altman would seem to be saying, "Why survive if not to extend the boundaries of our experience?   Why live on one
level of thought and action that only entails external possi-
bilities?"

For the filmmaker, form is the means of extending
these boundaries.   For his characters, a more meaningful
sense of community (a different social structure) would
serve a similar function.   Meanwhile, the viewer's simultaneous perception of the bisociative structures at work within both these levels may result in an integrative or "liber-
ating" experience.   This is what I assume left Pauline Kael
feeling so "elated. "   At the same time, Robin Wood's "de-
pression, " after seeing Nashville, can probably be located
in his failure to penetrate the core of Altman's bisociative
structure, because he only sees the "openness" (as synony-
mous with emptiness) that obscures it.   Or perhaps, to

paraphrase Mircea Eliade, many of Nashville's detractors
are afraid of confronting the "tyranny of open-endedness, "
which is, in fact, an extraordinarily apt designation for the
"hidden" subject of Nashville.


NOTES


[1]Robin Wood, "Smart-ass and Cutie-pie:   Notes
Toward an Evaluation of Robert Altman, " Movie 21, Autumn
1975, p. 5.
[2]Ibid. , pp. 11-12.
[3]Ibid. , p. 8.
[4]Ibid. , p. 9.
[5]Just as frequently, these surfaces create an aura of
uncertainty, which is linked to the very fabric of the text.
Because their use is so limited in M*A*S*H, I will have
more to say about this stylistic feature later on.
[6]Roger Greenspun, quoted in Judith M. Kass, Robert
Altman:   American Innovator (New York:   Popular Library,
1978), p. 18.
[7]An untitled interview in Film Comment, September-
October 1978, p. 18.
[8]Charles Schreger, "The Second Coming of Sound, "
Film Comment, September-October 1978, p. 35.
[9]Jonathan Rosenbaum, "Improvisations and Interactions in Altmanville, " Sight and Sound, Spring 1975, p. 91.
[10]Robert Altman, quoted in Kass, Robert Altman,
pp. 24-25.
[11]Untitled interview, Film Comment, September-
October 1978, p. 15.
[12]Ibid. , p. 16.
[13]Joan Tewkesbury, "Dialogue on Film, " American
Film, March 1979, p. 43.

# CHAPTER III

## GENRE AND MYTH

It is difficult to discuss narrative structure in Altman's films without relating the concept of narrativity to genre and myth. In the Western tradition, Giambattista Vico was one of the first to put forth a cyclical philosophy of history in which myth took on certain specific values. But it was not until Jung formulated the idea of mythic experience, manifesting itself in the archetypes of the collective unconscious, that its importance was recognized in relation to the arts. This is not intended to give full credit for modern acceptance of the value of myth to Jung but merely to acknowledge that he was able to provide a utilitarian framework upon which others could build.

Among Jung's many followers, Joseph Campbell has probably presented the relationship of narrativity to myth in the most comprehensive form. For Campbell, "It would not be too much to say that myth is the secret opening through which the inexhaustible energies of the cosmos pour into human cultural manifestations."[1] Campbell stresses the fact that in all cultures the mythological adventures of the hero follow a standard pattern, which he describes as "the nuclear unit of the monomyth." In a similar manner, Vladimir Propp's Morphology of the Folktale delineates the basic structural patterns or "functions" common to a large body of Russian folktales. But what differentiates Campbell from Propp is his Jungian propensity to explain the "meaning" of myth, as opposed to its structure. It is toward these ends that Campbell suggests that we understand the figures of ancient mythology not only as "symptoms of the unconscious," but as "intended" statements of certain fundamental spiritual principles.

Campbell asserts that the apprehension of this fundamental "universal doctrine" is frustrated "by the very organs through which the apprehension must be accomplished." In

other words, Campbell is merely reasserting the idea that
the essential unity of life is not recognizable by the ordinary
mind, in an ordinary state of consciousness.  For the ordinary (or nonintegrated) mind, refracted by the countless contradictions of human nature, must reflect the world as being
as diverse and confused as is humanity itself.  It is at this
point in his argument that Campbell's quasireligious interpretation takes on an added dimension of clarity:

> The function of ritual and myth is to make possi-
> ble, and then to facilitate, the jump--by analogy.
> Forms and conceptions that the mind and its
> senses can comprehend are presented and arranged
> in such a way as to suggest a truth or openness
> beyond.... Myth is but the penultimate; the ulti-
> mate is openness....  Therefore God and the gods
> are only convenient means--themselves of the na-
> ture of the world of names and forms....  They
> are mere symbols to move and awaken the mind,
> and to call it past themselves. [2]

Thus, although he attacks the problem from a completely
different direction, Campbell comes to a conclusion that is
similar to that of anthropologist Claude Lévi-Strauss with
regard to myth.  This conclusion, that mythic language takes
on different and more complex meanings according to context, is especially relevant in terms of Altman's open-ended
narrative strategies.

     Like mythic language, filmic language, which em-
bodies the modern myth of our culture, can also take on
different and more complex meanings.  In genre, which de-
velops, in part, out of the film industry's inherently entropic
nature, the myth is often commercially stereotyped to ensure
consumption.  What this usually entails is a reductive "disintegration" of meaning that precludes a positive synergistic
response on the part of the spectator.  As mentioned, the
dual nature of film as art and industry (with the emphasis
on "industry") results in the type of film that reinforces the
suspicions of its audience.  Genre aids in this process by
reducing or enclosing meaning within a set of conventions
that have already been assimilated by the collective consciousness of the audience.

     One of Altman's major achievements involves the ways
in which he has managed to reverse this process by subvert-
ing many of our traditional expectations from genre.  Taken

as a whole, his personal approach to genre also chronicles
a series of changes in the American national character,
from the adventurous, pioneering spirit of McCabe and Mrs.
Miller to the doomed sense of decay delineated in Quintet.
Along with these radically different visions of past and future,
Altman's genre films have variously sought to debunk the
myth of the western hero (Buffalo Bill and the Indians), portray the shift in mood from the pioneer days to the Depres-
sion (Thieves Like Us), and contrast earlier codes of morality with more contemporary sensibilities (The Long Goodbye,
A Perfect Couple).


## McCabe and Mrs. Miller (1971)


With McCabe and Mrs. Miller (1971), Altman proved
that his intensely "personal" (cf. modernist) approach to
filmmaking was eminently compatible with a traditional narrative structure.  Moreover, because McCabe and Mrs. Miller is deeply embedded in the general framework of the most
American of genres, Altman's deviations from the standard
western formulas take on added resonance.  In many ways
his most satisfying film, McCabe and Mrs. Miller's major
distinction lies in the way that Altman has managed to integrate many of his intuitive auteurist tendencies and quirks
(which, when unchecked, often detract from his other works)
into its overall structure.  Additionally, because this sense
of integration extends to nearly every level of the film's conception, one is not forced into the rather sticky, but generally justifiable, position of having to defend its flaws in the
light of more resounding achievements.

Instead of using "open spaces" as a means of engaging
its audience, McCabe and Mrs. Miller focuses on the demyth-
ification of the "open options" so central to the traditional
westerns of filmmakers like Howard Hawks and John Ford.
Using the western formula as a superficial, but nonetheless
essential, foundation, McCabe and Mrs. Miller virtually explodes the myth of the "American dream" in a way that
would not be possible in any other genre.  Sam Peckinpah
and Monte Hellman are two other directors who have used
the western as a springboard for their own personal life
views, but neither of them makes the kind of acute social
criticisms that Altman does.

A good deal of McCabe and Mrs. Miller's success

From McCabe and Mrs. Miller

rests with Altman's conception of his major characters.   Although John McCabe is a "dreamer," his hopes and aspirations are a natural outgrowth of the dramatic situation into
which he is thrust.   Despite the fact that the film's setting
(Washington, 1902) is already one generation removed from
the traditional western time frame, it still reeks of the
kinds of "impressions" that we have come to associate with
"open options."  Consequently, McCabe's characteristic lack
of self-knowledge can be romanticized without sacrificing
thematic resonance to the creation of emotional tension.

Equally important, the poignancy of McCabe's tragic-
comic heroism is heightened by his relationship to one of
Altman's most skillfully conceived "realists."   As portrayed
by Julie Christie, Mrs. Miller is an illusionless character
whose centrality to the narrative represents just one of the
many ways in which Altman veers off from traditional generic conventions.   Expanding her part from the Edward
Naughton novel (called only McCabe) upon which he and
Brian McKay based their screenplay, Altman's Mrs. Miller
adds some new wrinkles to the familiar figure of the "fallen
woman."  For, in spite of her aloofness, Mrs. Miller is
treated with so much sympathy and understanding that her

character eventually becomes as important to us as Warren
Beatty's McCabe. Undoubtedly, a great deal of her appeal
stems from her air of rugged independence and her ability
to carry on alone if need be. She is a survivor who has
learned how to control her emotions. What this results in
is a veritable reversal of traditional western roles, as
McCabe's naive buffoonery contrasts sharply with Mrs. Miller's silently accepting persona.

Stylistically, McCabe and Mrs. Miller utilizes a wide
range of techniques to support its typically bisociative themes.
Exemplifying what Pauline Kael termed Altman's apparently
"intuitive, quixotic, essentially impractical approach to movie-
making," the film only begins to reveal its structural complexity after repeated viewings. As Kael goes on to say (in
her New Yorker review, July 3, 1971), "A movie like this
isn't made by winging it; to improvise in a period setting
takes phenomenal discipline, but McCabe and Mrs. Miller
doesn't look 'disciplined,' as movies that lay everything out
for the audience do."

Certainly, McCabe and Mrs. Miller doesn't look disciplined in the way that a John Ford western does. Opening
with a high-angled pan that situates McCabe in an almost
dreamlike natural environment, Altman's subjective visual
style and contrapuntal use of sound offer subtle indications
of the way in which the director will attempt to infuse the
film with his own personal observations. But rather than
"lay everything out for the audience," the complexity of Altman's structural strategy is underscored by the use of Leonard Cohen's enigmatic lyrics ("he was just a Joseph looking
for a manger") over McCabe's initial entrance into the town
of Presbyterian Church. For as soon as he emerges from
the misty woods, it is quite evident that what McCabe is
really looking for is a place to earn a quick buck. Moreover, because his demeanor and appearance are atypical of
the traditional western hero, it is difficult for the audience
to decide how to react to McCabe.

One way to read McCabe's character is provided by
the immediate impression that his arrival creates among the
film's inner audience. After entering the primitive saloon
owned by Sheehan (Rene Auberjonois), McCabe sets off a
nonstop stream of overlapping dialogue that reflects the little mining community's provincialism. Because none of the
men are wearing firearms, McCabe's "Swedish" gun attracts
an inordinate amount of attention. Similarly, although what

Leonard Cohen's lyrics refer to as "the holy game of poker"
already seems to be Presbyterian Church's favorite pastime,
the locals are overly anxious to try their hands against this
glib "professional" who drinks from a silver flask and covers
the gaming table with a bright red cloth.

McCabe's charismatic charm is heightened by his cocky
sense of humor.  When Sheehan publicly confronts him with
his supposed reputation as a gunfighter--who killed someone
named Bill Roundtree--McCabe neither confirms nor denies
it, preferring to come back with a typical one-liner ("What's
the matter, Sheehan, you got a turd up your ass?").  Thus,
when Sheehan insists on telling anyone who will listen that
"Pudgy" McCabe's got a "big rep, " we get the feeling that
the townsfolk enjoy nurturing this rumor as a way to brighten
up their dreary existence.  Meanwhile, McCabe is astute
enough to know a good thing when he sees it, and it is not
long before he parlays this knowledge with a little business
venture that ironically establishes him as one of Presbyterian Church's leading citizens.

In addition to his use of sound, Altman also exploits
the structural potential of color and lighting throughout these
early scenes.  Because he wanted to create a mood of nostal-
gia or "reminiscence" for the period, Altman tried as much
as possible to use original sources (oil lamps) for all his
interiors.  Then, during the shooting of McCabe, Altman decided to give the film an antique brown quality.  As Tommy
Thompson tells it, "He walked around with a Polaroid camera and an off-yellow velour sweatshirt.  It was the old
Polaroid, that you had to pull the film out.  He would take
a picture of his shirt at the stomach, of this yellow, and
pull it out to be developed.  He was flashing the film (ex-
posing it to light) is what he was doing.  And it would have
that yellow, brown overtone on it...."3

Ultimately, these warm brown hues take on thematic
overtones as they become associated with the community's
desire for domestic security amidst their hostile natural environment.  In a similar way, Altman pays a great deal of
attention to the town's underdeveloped qualities in order to
point out the vast potential ("open options") that appears to
exist here.  For as the film progresses, Altman will use
Presbyterian Church's transformation from a shabby little
settlement as one of the film's major thematic motifs.  Consequently, because it is McCabe who is chiefly responsible
for the town's burgeoning growth, he rapidly becomes a
force to be reckoned with.

The real key to McCabe's (and the town's) unlikely success is the result of a clever variation on the theme of frontier ingenuity. It is not long before McCabe manages to procure three "chippies" from the neighboring town of Bearpaw, who will form the base for his expanding business operations. At the same time, the construction boom that marks McCabe's reentry to Presbyterian Church offers visual proof of the viability of his present undertaking. Shrewdly surmising the situation, Sheehan quickly proposes a partnership that would help them to eliminate any unwanted competition. However, because things have been going so well up to this point, McCabe turns him down without so much as a second thought. Then, as if to undermine McCabe's illusory assumption of control, Altman interjects an appropriate Leonard Cohen lyric over a flash cut to one of McCabe's whores, as she inexplicably rushes out and stabs an unidentified client.

In effect, this action serves to set the stage for the belated arrival of Mrs. Miller. Unlike Sheehan, she is hardly awed by what she mockingly terms McCabe's "frontier wit," and actually scores points when she tells him, "If you want to make out you're such a fancy dude, you ought to stop using that cheap Jockey Club cologne." Astonished by her adroitness, McCabe is finally won over by Mrs. Miller's offer of partnership when she points out his ignorance on such pivotal matters as feminine hygiene and bordello management. Also, because the main thrust of her argument is that McCabe thinks "too small," Mrs. Miller's immediate impact on the town is as profound as McCabe's. This is borne out by both the rapidity and the detail with which Altman focuses upon the construction of the new bathhouse that is erected at her instigation.

In fact, with a minimum of exposition, Altman succeeds in establishing Mrs. Miller's influence on the collective psyche of the community to such a degree that McCabe soon finds himself having to remind the men that he's still the boss. As the town continues to grow by leaps and bounds, Altman's narrative alternates between McCabe and Mrs. Miller's growing relationship and the sense of community that seems to derive largely from their joint enterprise. Concurrently, this portion of the film touches upon peripheral details that round out our impressions of the town. Among the most noteworthy of these is the arrival of Bart Coyle's mail-order bride, which is followed by the appearance of some new girls whom Mrs. Miller has summoned from Seattle.

The completely segregated Chinese section of town is
also glimpsed here, and the memory of its separateness imbues Jeremy Berg's subsequent anecdote with an ironic tinge.
Jeremy's "Chinese Princess" story ("It's true, a guy I know
spent $5.00 just to find out") exemplifies one of the many
ways that Altman links his inner audience's quest for a sense
of community with the excitement generated by McCabe and
Mrs. Miller's ongoing efforts.    However, the implicit irony
of this sequence stems from the way that Altman utilizes its
dreamlike qualities to sum up the paradox of a community
founded upon illusion and exploitation.    Thus, although Altman has been able to romanticize the community's development in a way that would not be possible in his depictions
of an industrialized America, he also gives us pause to
doubt that the concept of inner-direction was ever a viable
one in this country.

This primary theme is most fully explored in conjunction with the rise and fall of McCabe's own personal fortunes.
At the same time, however, its effectiveness at the emotional level can be seen as a direct result of his relationship
with Mrs. Miller.    For it is through this relationship that
Altman most clearly reveals the sense of vulnerability that
enables McCabe to achieve the stature of a tragic hero.
Once again, Altman accomplishes this by making Mrs. Miller every bit as stubborn as McCabe.    Thus, although the
two are obviously attracted to one another, they both possess too much pride to admit their real emotions.    But
whereas Mrs. Miller silently endures her painful isolation,
McCabe is subject to fits of (often comical) frustration that
deflate his cocky pretensions.

Consequently, when Mrs. Miller is requested by a
client, in the presence of McCabe, he is driven to total distraction, while she is able to perform her duty without blink-
ing a lash.    In the very next scene, Altman intercuts Mrs.
Miller's silent (except for Cohen on the soundtrack) walk
through the snowy night with McCabe's unsuccessful attempts
to do some bookkeeping.    The implication (heightened by
Cohen's lyrics) is that she has come to calm her lover down.
But, in keeping with their volatile temperaments, Altman
turns the scene into a heated clash of wills that says a great
deal about their respective characters.

McCabe's ego is fragile.    He suffers from a lack of
foresight.    McCabe wants Mrs. Miller to stay away from the
books, despite her superior aptitude for accounting.    Clearly,

his argument (that he can "hold his own in any game of chance") reveals his lack of self-knowledge. She counters that he thinks too small, and goes on to disclose an entirely pragmatic plan to eventually open a "proper boarding house" in San Francisco. She has no illusions. Because of their differences, they quarrel and he sulks.

Unlike Mrs. Miller, McCabe's major problem involves his failure to recognize his limitations. Thus, when the agents from a large mining company come to buy him out, he is guilty of overplaying his most crucial hand. Skillfully interweaving this sequence of events with McCabe's renewed efforts to impress Mrs. Miller, Altman handles the whole affair in a manner that calls for some detailed analysis. Still seething from his recent tiff with Mrs. Miller, McCabe greets the agents (Michael Murphy and Anthony Holland) from Harrison & Shaughnessy with an overabundance of arrogance. Preoccupied with his attempts to reaffirm his self-image, McCabe brushes aside their initial offer with the same smart-ass quip that had worked earlier on Sheehan ("If a frog had wings, he wouldn't bump his ass so much").

But since Murphy and Holland have already bought Sheehan out, it is obvious that the current situation demands a good deal more consideration than McCabe can presently muster. For, instead of cultivating the agents' interest, he wanders off alone to get drunk in the baths. Now Altman cuts between McCabe and a birthday party for one of his whores, where his absence is duly noted. Perhaps prompted by this, Mrs. Miller leaves the party to take refuge in her heretofore undisclosed opium habit. Before she can indulge herself, McCabe comes calling with a bouquet of flowers. She asks him if he's bathed, whereupon he begins to brag about how he plans to bilk the agents from Harrison & Shaughnessy. Coolly reflected in a mirror, Mrs. Miller sagely replies that he better hope they come back because "they'd just as soon put a bullet in you." McCabe, however, just can't admit that he's in over his head.

Mrs. Miller's tacit acknowledgment of the ramifications of these circumstances is most strikingly revealed by the way that Altman cuts from McCabe's refusal of Murphy's subsequent, and more generous, offer, to a reverse zoom of her lighting up her opium pipe. In this way, Mrs. Miller distances herself from McCabe's further blunderings, while he goes on to seal his fate by mentioning a highly inflated figure that he evidently intends to readjust in the morning.

Due to his lack of tact, however, there will be no further
negotiations.    This fact is presaged by McCabe's next encounter with the zonked-out Mrs. Miller.    Zooming in on
her (as Cohen sings on the soundtrack), Altman again uses
this bittersweet interlude to underscore the parallelism between their ill-fated romance and McCabe's mistaken assessment of his bargaining position.    Thus, as McCabe climbs
into bed, Mrs. Miller's silent request for her fee precipi-
tates an ironic zoom-in to her money box, which deflates his
actions even further.    Accordingly, when Altman returns to
Murphy and Holland, we are already prepared for their decision to give up on McCabe.

From this point on, the entire mood of the film
changes radically.    After McCabe has made his fatal mistake, it appears that all there is left to do is build toward
the inevitable showdown.    Consequently, when a lone rider
(Keith Carradine) approaches Bart Coyle's funeral gathering,
both the timing and the tone seem to argue for a traditional
confrontation.    Instead, Altman actually mocks this conven-
tion by turning the scene into just one of a series of protracted sequences that will allow him to develop his various
themes further.    After McCabe and the young stranger square
off, Altman employs a portentous zoom-in to the young man,
only to reveal that he has come in search of Presbyterian
Church's fabled whorehouse.

At the same time, Altman attempts to maintain some
suspense by cutting directly to a new trio of riders.    Moreover, because he zooms out from this subsequent shot, the
very symmetry of Altman's compositions add yet another
texture to his abrupt shifts in mood.    In this case (as in
most of McCabe), Altman's use of the zoom functions as a
stylistic device that brings the viewer into the narrative, as
opposed to its more "overt" or self-reflexive function of
distanciation, as employed in other of his films.    In other
words, because McCabe is not as dependent on the creation
of structural ambiguity as a means of engaging its audience
(as opposed to Nashville or any one of Altman's "dream"
films), Altman's personal style in this film is less likely to
call attention to itself.    The result is a visual style that
lends itself to comparisons with such impressionist painters
as Degas, and the early still photographers whose dynamic
compositions were often imitated by the Impressionists.
This harkens back to the notion of the nostalgic or "reminiscent" qualities of Altman's images, achieved by combining diffused natural lighting with the use of highly stylized

composition and period detail. Among the many scenes that
fit this description, Altman's depiction of an old man dancing
on the ice to the accompaniment of several local musicians
is particularly revealing of his skillful evocation of an era. [4]
But, like the Degasesque bath scene that was intercut with
the story of the "Chinese Princess," Altman invariably uses
these images for a definite narrative purpose. In the present instance, this entails another deflation of the community's
sense of security, as the arrival of the three gunmen sent by
Harrison & Shaughnessy sends the merrymakers scurrying
for shelter.

Aside from Mrs. Miller, no one in the town has very
much to say to McCabe once his fortunes begin to change.
But when she advises him to leave town while there's still
time, he foolishly insists that there's no reason to run away.
As soon as he comes face to face with the gargantuan Butler
(Hugh Millais) and his two sidekicks, Breed and the Kid,
however, McCabe's confident façade is irrevocably undercut.
This is accomplished when Butler's attempts to provoke a
fight with McCabe result in the latter's virtual admission
that he never really did shoot Bill Roundtree. Then, as if
to put McCabe's "big rep" to rest once and for all, Altman
zooms in to Butler as he tells Sheehan that McCabe "never
killed anyone in his life."

Regardless of the problems that surround him,
McCabe's thoughts never stray far from Mrs. Miller. This
is most poignantly revealed in an ensuing soliloquy, during
which McCabe tells the absent Mrs. Miller that "I've got
poetry in me." Ironically, this speech, which underscores
McCabe's limitations more emphatically than any other portion of the film, also imbues McCabe's character with an
enormous amount of new-found sympathy. And it is by baring the soul of one of "humanity's most vulnerable members,"
that Altman sharpens his focus on the complex issue of heroic individualism. For, in order that McCabe's plight achieve
greater thematic and emotional resonance, Altman finds it
necessary to first demythify (or humanize) his tragic hero.
Having done this, Altman has finally arrived at the point
where his sociopolitical observations can carry their full
weight.

This mixture of personal and societal issues all
comes together in a brief scene that takes place in the town
of Bearpaw. Unable to locate Murphy and Holland, with
whom he hopes he can still strike a deal, McCabe enters

the law office of one Clement Samuels (William Devane).  It
is here that McCabe falls prey to the myth of open options,
a myth already crumbling before his very eyes.  Largely because of his need to prove his self-worth to Mrs. Miller,
McCabe latches onto a line of moralistic rhetoric (the "American dream") that even he cannot quite believe in.  But all
that we (and McCabe) have just witnessed gives a hollow ring
to Devane's flamboyant defense of a man who "goes into the
wilderness and builds an enterprise with his own hands. "
Nevertheless, McCabe is rapidly running out of options and
the idea of becoming "a hero" by "busting up trusts and
monopolies" sounds pretty good to him, as expressed by this
smooth-talking lawyer with lofty political ambitions (Devane
fancies himself as "the next senator from the state").

Having returned to Presbyterian Church, McCabe is
next seen trying to impress Mrs. Miller with his new-found
calling as the protector of the small businessman.  But as
she is well aware, the specter of Harrison & Shaughnessy's
three hired assassins can result in only one kind of struggle.
In this respect, Mrs. Miller's fatalism is duly substantiated
by the way that the Kid ruthlessly guns down Keith Carradine
in the very next sequence.  This action is followed by
McCabe and Mrs. Miller's most moving love scene, which
is highlighted by McCabe's near breakdown after Mrs. Miller invites him into bed for the first time without asking for
her fee.  The emotional impact of this meeting is further
enhanced by both its proximity to Carradine's recent death
and the inevitability of McCabe's own impending confrontation.

Although McCabe and Mrs. Miller is riddled with
irony, Altman saves the crowning touch for the very end.
On one level, it is expressed by having McCabe enact the
traditional hero's role.  For, not only does he stand up to
the three gunmen, he actually manages to defeat all three.
In the end, however, McCabe's heroism is completely
stripped of its traditional meaning because it has absolutely
no effect on the community itself.  Moreover, by intercutting
McCabe's struggle with the town's efforts to put out a fire in
the church, Altman shrewdly debunks the myth of the frontier
society's ability to band together in the face of crisis.  Although the townsfolk do finally come together, it is not to
save their leading member, whose fight remains totally ig-
nored, but rather to rescue a symbolic structure whose true
meaning and function in their lives has long been forgotten.

The showdown itself is a long, drawn-out affair that

shares many basic similarities with Gary Cooper's climactic
stand in High Noon.   Using a series of point-of-view shots
(many of them zooms) for the first time in the film, Altman
subtly encourages the viewer to identify more and more
strongly with McCabe as he succeeds in picking off the first
two assassins, Breed and the Kid.   During this action, the
steadily increasing snowfall orchestrates a powerful visual
crescendo, which peaks just after the last shot is fired.
Having killed his three adversaries, the mortally wounded
McCabe is then juxtaposed to the jubilant townsfolk, who
have just put out the fire, in Altman's last jibe at their
empty sense of triumph.

        Fittingly, the film's closing shots take place in the
Chinese ghetto--the neglected underbelly of Presbyterian
Church.   Here, Altman intercuts a zoom-in to the stoned-
out Mrs. Miller with a corresponding zoom-in to the body
of her lover, all but obscured by the blowing snow.   In this
way, the grainy quality of McCabe's fading image provides a
perfect parallel to Mrs. Miller's fogged-out state of survival, as the film ends with a zoom-in to an extreme close-up
of Mrs. Miller's heretofore impenetrable eye.   Ultimately,
then, Altman winds up by reinforcing the inherent romanticism of his tragic love story, without having to compromise
his indictment of the "American dream."   Despite their
flaws, we have come to care about McCabe and Mrs. Miller
in a way that not only supplements Altman's broader themes,
but also rounds out the dramatic context that makes those
themes worth pondering.


                    Buffalo Bill and the Indians,  or
                Sitting Bull's History Lesson (1976)


        Because it lacks the sense of tension between realism
and romanticism that distinguishes McCabe and Mrs. Miller,
Buffalo Bill and the Indians runs the risk of failing to engage
its audience beyond the level of its intellectual pyrotechnics.
Rather than using the traditional western formula as a springboard for his own world view (cf. the "antiwesterns" of Sam
Peckinpah or Monte Hellman), Altman's adaptation of Arthur
Kopit's play is such a merciless debunking of the western
myth that it is difficult to even consign it to the western
genre.   But then again, because the modern western, as we
know it, is largely derived from dime novels and Wild West

From Buffalo Bill and the Indians

Shows, of which Buffalo Bill's was by far the most famous, there is more than ample reason for examining the film in this context.

Unlike his fictionalized protagonist, Altman has never been one to assert that the "truth is whatever gets the loudest applause." Nor is Buffalo Bill and the Indians concerned with the kind of truth that results from exhaustive historical research. Instead, Altman has attempted to fashion a quasi-philosophical inquiry into the nature of truth in relationship to certain mythologized misconceptions about the American past. In the process, Altman not only deflates the ostensible heroics of one of our most revered historical figures, but also uses an essentially self-reflexive show-business motif to imply that our present-day film industry still tends to support Bill's credo.

As befits Altman's Bicentennial film (although Nashville deals with the Bicentennial, it was made and released in 1975), Buffalo Bill and the Indians opens with the raising of the American flag. The setting is the tent community belonging to William F. Cody's Wild West Show, 1885. Following the title ("Robert Altman's Absolutely Unique and Heroic Enterprise of Inimicable Lustre!"), which informs us

of the film's debunking tone, the camera pans to an old soldier.   As he tells us that the events we are about to witness
are part of the making of the American frontier, an Indian
raid is enacted (credits appear over this).   Emphasizing the
Indians' savagery, the raid is accompanied by the music of
Buffalo Bill's Cowboy Band.   Then, as a voice yells, "Cease
the action!   From the beginning," we suddenly realize that
what we have been watching is a rehearsal for the show.

Partly to reinforce the obvious filmmaking parallels
inherent in this opening sequence, Altman cuts directly to
Ned Buntline (Burt Lancaster) as he tells a saloon keeper
how he made Cody a "star."   Bitterly sarcastic, Buntline
functions in the film as a sort of Greek chorus.   Accordingly, this early speech also makes us aware of the fact that
Cody is guilty of forgetting where he got his start, but Cody's
real problems go far deeper than this.   Because he is a legend in his own time, William F. "Buffalo Bill" Cody is faced
with the enormous burden of trying to live up to his myth.
Consequently, Bill seems tailor-made for Altman's basic
auteurist structure wherein the protagonist's initial assumption of control is gradually revealed as illusory.   However,
since Bill is already a helpless victim of his illusion when
the film begins, Altman is forced to begin tearing him down
from the very outset.

Unlike McCabe, whose personal dilemma could be in-
flected, for the sake of emotional identification, without sacrificing thematic resonance, Buffalo Bill is allowed no such
outlet.   In other words, because Buffalo Bill and the Indians's
chief thrust is dependent on turning Bill into a symbol of our
society's propensity for perpetuating cruel and harmful myths
about our culture, Altman can ill afford to romanticize his
present protagonist.   Thus, instead of attempting to generate
audience identification as a means of engaging the viewer (as
in McCabe), Buffalo Bill and the Indians's overriding thematic
concerns dictate a much more polemical approach to its subject matter.   What this results in approximates the ultimate
subversion of our expectations from the western genre, as
the film's major battles are fought with words instead of
guns.   Moreover, whenever traditional dramatic elements
are allowed to surface, they are invariably used to further
diminish Bill's character.

Although Bill is at its center, his entire Wild West
Show--"America's National Family"--shares the brunt of
Altman's attack.   Among the show's members, Nate Alsbury

(Joel Grey), the producer, and Major "Arizona" John Burke
(Kevin McCarthy), the publicist, are by far the most repre-
hensible. When they are not busy dreaming up new ways to
distort the truth, these two profit-mongering sycophants spend
most of their time smoothing over their meal ticket's increasing inability to differentiate his legend from reality. Proudly
proclaiming that he's going to "Codyfy" the world, Nate is
sent to get rid of Buntline, because Bill lacks the courage to
face up to his creator. But after cutting the rug out from
under Nate's feet ("When two partners always agree, one of
'em ain't necessary), Buntline makes it clear that he's not
leaving until Bill asks him to personally.

Meanwhile, Paul Newman plays Bill as a self-deluded
con man who drinks his booze by the schooner as he awaits
the arrival of his newest attraction, Chief Sitting Bull. Without a doubt, Sitting Bull and his interpreter, William Halsey
(Will Sampson), are the real heroes of the film. Bull is a
small, quiet man, whose dignified silence serves as a perfect counterpart to Bill's verbosity. Halsey, on the other
hand, is large in stature (which causes Bill to mistake him
for Bull), and extremely articulate. His opening lines,
which refer to Bull's "incarceration," have the immediate
effect of befuddling Bill, who leans over to ask Burke what
the Indian means. Bill's reaction here is doubly ironic,
given his own (and Nate and Burke's) proclivity for the ostentatious misuse of his native tongue. Furthermore, his
rejoinder, that Halsey is a white name ("You got a little
white blood in ya?") introduces the film's central motif of
oneupmanship between the Indians and whites.

Because Bull is also a legend in his own time, Altman ensures that Bill's distorted sense of truth cannot be
exonerated on account of his circumstances. In a similar
vein, the major irony of Buffalo Bill and the Indians' con-
tinual series of confrontations is that the "dreamers" (Bull
and Halsey) rather than the "realists" (Bill and his aides)
see life as it really is. For example, Bill and his entour-
age are sure that Bull can't cross a nearby river, simply
because they themselves have already failed to do so. Then,
when Bull accomplishes the crossing with incredible ease,
Bill tries to wriggle out of his embarrassment by insisting
that the far side of the river "is exactly where I want him."
In an ensuing sequence of events, Halsey's request for
blankets for the Sioux is granted by Nate because he sees
it as an inexpensive publicity ploy. But when Halsey says
that Bull wants to be paid six weeks' salary in advance, Nate

balks at his request for "prevancement." Even more incredible to Nate's way of thinking, Bull will not sign a contract
since he only intends to stay until he sees the "Great Father," whom his dreams have told him he will meet at the
show. As usual, a compromise is finally arrived at just
before the next confrontation. This occurs while the troop
is rehearsing Custer's last stand, just after Nate has attempted to regale Bull with his company's courage in pre-
senting history "without taking sides." But when Bull's
"colored" stand-in shoots Custer in the back, Halsey informs Nate that Bull wasn't even present on the battlefield.
In this instance, the Indians clearly come out on top, as
the scene ends with Bull's public exposure of Bill's remarkable marksmanship--which is achieved with the aid of a
"scattergun."

Shortly thereafter, Bill, who's taken off his long
blond wig, informs his latest in a long line of opera-singing
paramours--his major concession to culture--that she had
better leave so he can devote his full attention to Bull. The
next morning, Halsey wakes the wigless Bill to tell him of
the (real) scene Bull wants to perform. Humiliated at first,
Bill covers his head with a blanket as he strains to remain
calm while listening to Halsey's proposal "to show how the
cowardly white man does not fight unless it is against wom-
en or old people or children." But when he begins to reply
to Bull, his sense of indignation steadily builds until he
screams out, "You're fired!" Bill would probably stick to
his decision, too, were it not for the fact (the profit motive)
that Annie Oakley (Geraldine Chaplin) threatens to leave if
Bull is sent off.

In this way, Buffalo Bill and the Indians proceeds in
a series of set pieces in which the Indians increasingly begin to gain the upper hand. For even Bull's first attempt
at performing in "the show business" undercuts Bill's over-
confident expectations. Bill, as he tells it to Halsey, fully
expects the chief to be sorry that he didn't do his Custer
act after Bull suffers the humiliation of the crowd. And at
first, Bill's hopes appear to be justified as Bull's simple
entrance is greeted by jeers and laughter. But as he continues to ride slowly around the arena, Bull's quiet sense
of dignity turns the crowd's wrath into cheers. Here again,
Altman seems to be making a subtle self-reflexive reference
to his own profession, for this scene implies that there are
numerous--and often more meaningful--ways to achieve success other than strict adherence to traditional dramatic conventions.

On the other hand, it could be argued that <u>Buffalo
Bill and the Indians</u> suffers from a tendency to stereotype
both Indians and whites, which greatly reduces its impact.
Certainly, the film's glorification of Halsey and Bull (in
conjunction with its episodic structure) results in a fair
amount of redundancy.  Similarly, Bill and his retinue are
such outrageous caricatures that we may soon lose interest
in their antics.  Then, too, the film's polemical tone tends
to affect the sort of trendy liberalism that makes one wonder if it has any meaning for the viewer who is not already
firmly convinced of its ideological precepts.  Together with
its basically static qualities, this last point suggests that
<u>Buffalo Bill and the Indians</u> was eminently more suited to
the stage, where it was called only <u>Indians</u> and where it
could rely more on the sharpness and immediacy of its dialogue to carry the evening.

Although there is a lot of truth in these criticisms,
Altman and his collaborators nearly manage to overcome
them.  For one thing, despite some black marks on his
escutcheon, Buffalo Bill is anything but an easy target for
satire.  His myth is too strong.  For another, the casting
of Paul Newman, with his boyish charm so typical of Altman's protagonists (think of Elliott Gould, Donald Sutherland,
George Segal, Bud Cort, Warren Beatty, and Keith Carradine), adds a definite countercurrent to Altman's debunking.
Even more important, most of the film's individual scenes
of confrontation possess enough inventiveness, in terms of
both style and conception, to mitigate against its various in-
consistencies and excesses.  In other words, in spite of its
flaws, the film combines an innovative, albeit hardly "open,"
treatment of highly laudable themes with--for want of a better phrase--a high level of entertainment.  The only catch is
that it's a different (because it is bisociative) type of entertainment than we have come to expect from the western genre.

In order to supplement these observations with specific examples, it is well worth considering several other of the
film's more successful sequences.  While trying to come on to
his newest opera singer, Lucille, Bill discovers that Bull and
his braves are riding off.  He sends Buck Taylor, the show's
trick rider, across the river to check things out, but Buck
is separated from his horse.  More humor is derived from
Bill's own preparation to give chase, as he clumsily knocks
over the cage of Lucille's pet canary (Bill hates birds) after
rummaging about for his "real" jacket.  Once Bill's posse
sets off in pursuit of the Indians, Altman subverts our tra-

ditional expectation from genre in two distinct ways.  Not
only does Bill come back empty-handed, but the chase itself
is never shown.   Here Altman characteristically opts for
ironic commentary over physical action:  the chase is replaced with a brief scene in which Buntline debunks Bill with
yet another witticism.

When Bill comes back, Altman underscores his confusion and loss of pride with a zoom-in to Bill while he
looks up at his portrait, as if to apologize to his heroic
image.   Then, after he silently retires to his bedroom and
some shots are heard, Bill's aides rush in, fearing the
worst.   But it is only Cody shooting wildly at Lucille's
canary, which has escaped from its cage.   With the abrupt
reappearance of Halsey and Bull, Bill's image takes a further pounding, which he tries to alleviate by denying that
he ever tried to catch up with them.   The next scene then
makes another comment on Bill's manner of distorting truth
as Buntline, in front of a mirror, says that responsibility
is different for stars than for ordinary folk.   "That's why
stars spend so much time in front of the mirror, seeing if
their good looks and word delivery can overcome their
judgment. "  Finally, the sequence ends with a cut to Bill,
in front of the mirror, practicing his excuses for not finding Bull.

Racism is another prominent motif, which is integrated into the episode involving the taking of the Wild
West's publicity photo.   Noting that Bull is standing next to
Annie, Bill stops the photographer and passes this information on to Nate.   Nate informs Burke, who asks Halsey to
tell Bull to move.   Halsey says that Bull will move for
twenty-five dollars, whereupon Bill comes up with the idea
that they can simply doctor the photo if taken as is.   A
moment later, the session is interrupted by a telegraph an-
nouncing that President Cleveland intends to celebrate his
honeymoon at Bill's Wild West camp.   As everyone except
Halsey and Bull rushes off toward the telegraph office, Halsey tells the photographer that he can "take the picture now."
Still later, Bill will add to this racist motif by telling one
of his servile black troopers that it's "too bad Injuns ain't
learned a thing from you coloreds. "

Meanwhile, Buntline sums up the present action by
telling his barroom audience that "things are startin' to take
on an unreal shape. "  Reiterating the fact that Bull's dream
has come true, he goes on to say that "Bill can't believe in

somebody else's dream 'cause he don't have none of his own,
so there's no way he's fully prepared to understand what has
taken place. " This speech occurs over a zoom-in to the
President's box at Bill's "first after-dark request performance. " Consistent with his deflation of all our great white
heroes, with the possible exception of Annie, Altman wastes
little time in cutting the President (Pat McCormick) down to
size. Thus, after Burke tries to enhance the effect of one
of Bill's "Codyisms" by telling the President that Bill writes
all his own material, Cleveland finds it necessary to consult
one of his aides, Fizician, before coming back with the re-
sultingly self-deprecating reply, "All great men do. "

The highlight of the show is undoubtedly Bull's new
act, in which he is going to make his gray horse dance.
But when Bull enters the arena, Altman insets an auspicious
zoom-in to Halsey, as if to warn us that something particularly momentous is about to happen. Pursuant to this, Bull
points his gun directly at the President, but raises it in the
air before firing. The gray mare now begins to dance, and
the President's group responds with nervous laughter. Here
again, Burke chimes in by assuring the President that it's
all part of the act.

In contrast to Buffalo Bill's Wild West, which symbolizes the shallowness of the "American dream, " Sitting Bull's
attitude toward dreams provides Altman with a particularly
apt metaphor for inner-direction. Similarly, the outcome of
Bull's meeting with the President (the outcome of his dreams)
constitutes one of Altman's strongest indictments of the way
that authentic spiritual experience has been rendered useless
by the hypocrisy of the system. When Cleveland repeatedly
insists that Bull's request is "out of the question" without
even taking the time to hear it, Bull is unceremoniously
stripped of his main reason for living. But even here, Altman cannot resist further embellishing the scene with some
additional, deflationary dialogue. Accordingly, Bill congrat-
ulates Cleveland by telling him that "the difference between
Presidents and chiefs in a situation like this is a President
knows enough to retaliate before it's his turn. " Finally,
after Bill offers the newlyweds his bed for the evening (Bill
maintains that he's going to sleep out under the stars), the
scene ends with Cleveland's ironic reply: "It's men like you
who have made this country what it is, Buffalo Bill. "

Feeling lonely and ill at ease, Bill later decides to
visit the bar where Buntline has been holding court. Yet

even in his present state, Bill can't seem to stop himself
from manipulating the truth.    This is emphasized by a zoom-
in to Bill as he blames Nate for his own failure to make
further use of Ned's talents.    Having seen Bill in the flesh
once more, however, Buntline has no more reason to hang
around.    So, after telling Bill that it was the thrill of his
life to have invented him, Buntline rides off, leaving Bill
alone in the night.

From this point on, Bill is never quite the same.
When we next see him, one year later, Bill is drinking more
and enjoying it less.    He's also taken to repeating himself
quite a bit, a habit that does not go unnoticed by his staff.
Appropriately, Bill's climactic separation from reality occurs
just after the news arrives (although Bill doesn't know about
it yet) that Sitting Bull has been killed while trying to escape
from the reservation at Standing Rock.    Cutting from a shot
of Bill performing to a slow zoom-in on Bull's grave, Altman imbues this sequence with a dreamlike quality by cutting
immediately back to Bill as he wakes up in the bedroom.
In his drunken delirium, Bill's belief that he sees Bull in
his conference room (shades of Macbeth) sparks a lengthy
soliloquy in which he pathetically attempts to reaffirm his
own myth.

In the end, however, life (or the "show") goes on as
usual, as Altman cuts from Bill's soliloquy to a performance
in which he subdues the mighty Sitting Bull, now played by
Halsey.    But as the camera zooms in to an extreme close-
up of Bill, his crazed expression makes it clear that the
man's legend has extracted its toll.    As the crowd roars its
approval, Altman heightens this vision of isolated illusion by
cutting to a long shot (end credits begin) before pulling his
camera back for a final bird's-eye glimpse of this world of
make-believe.

## Thieves Like Us (1974)

Altman has spoken of Thieves Like Us as a look at
another generation of Americans, thirty years after McCabe.
However, as a "document of America at that time," Thieves
Like Us manifests a curious blend of realism and overt
structural strategies, which underscore Altman's personal
approach to his material.    Moreover, in his depiction of

From Thieves Like Us

Depression-ridden America in the 1930s, Altman is once
again (cf. Brewster McCloud, McCabe and Mrs. Miller, The
Long Goodbye, California Split) drawn to a group of outsiders, who constitute the focal point of his narrative.  Essentially a "gangster" film, Thieves Like Us has its main point
of generic departure in the director's refusal to romanticize
either his heroes or their exploits.  And, while this refusal
undoubtedly goes a long way toward explaining the film's disappointing reception at the box office, it also helps to make
Thieves Like Us a refreshingly original treatment of its subject matter.

Although it is based on the same Edward Anderson
novel that served as the source of Nicholas Ray's They Live
by Night (1949), Altman's version is strikingly unique. 5  Set
in the thirties with a great deal of attention to period detail
(Ray's film had a contemporary setting), Thieves's use of
naturalistic lighting and color provides a sharp contrast to
the high-key lighting and studio-bound sets that characterize
They Live by Night (and most other films noirs).  Other
stylistic differences that set Thieves apart from various
films of this genre include the impression of improvisation
created by its performers and the innovative use of sound.
Finally, Altman's penchant for using moving-camera shots,
instead of direct cuts, is consistent with his usual movement
away from the classical Hollywood visual style.

In addition to its unconventional narrative strategy of
downplaying action in favor of a series of unexpected domestic scenes, Thieves Like Us contrasts this "reality" with the
dramatic myths upon which the main characters' dreams are
based.  In this sense, Thieves Like Us is very much about
communications and the media's ability to influence the public's behavior patterns.  Accordingly, because society in the
thirties is already seen to be on the road to mass conformity, Altman can no longer romanticize the plight of his self-
deluded dreamers, as he did in McCabe and Mrs. Miller.
Instead, their attempts to improve their lot in life, by rob-
bing banks, is portrayed as a rather aimless and absurd
means of existence, which is in no way compensated for by
the heroic overtones that inflect McCabe.

The three bank robbers in Thieves Like Us all fit into Altman's basic structural pattern of rise and fall.  Among
them, Bowie (Keith Carradine) is the most central because
his youthful innocence would seem to afford him the greatest
chance to survive.  In the end, however, even Bowie is

defeated because he cannot adjust to the realities of the system. Another familiar pattern in the film is the way the thieves are played off against more realistic types whose lack of self-delusions ensures that they will survive. In Thieves, Mattie (Louise Fletcher) is particularly representative of this other type, while Keechie (Shelley Duvall) is a somewhat more pathetic version. Thus, although Keechie makes the mistake of falling in love with Bowie, her awareness of her own limitations prevents her from sharing in his fate. Unlike Cathy O'Donnell in They Live by Night, Duvall's Keechie also contributes to Thieves's antiromantic tone by demonstrating the failure of love to mediate against the insurmountable web of circumstances that ensnare the hero.

Thieves's use of many of Altman's "repertory" performers (Keith Carradine, Shelley Duvall, John Schuck, Bert Remsen, and Tom Skerritt) lends the film a familiar sense of presence, as does the behind-the-scenes work done by such long-time Altman associates as Joan Tewkesbury (cowriter), Lou Lombardo (editor), Robert Eggenweiler (associate producer), and Tommy Thompson (assistant director). But one of the more remarkable aspects of Thieves Like Us is that, despite the rare absence of production designer Leon Erickson and cinematographer Vilmos Zsigmond, who worked on Altman's three previous films (McCabe, Images, and The Long Goodbye), this film's visual style is extremely close to that of Altman's other works. The main conclusion to be drawn from this is, as Tommy Thompson puts it, that Altman "knows that camera. He knows lenses, filters, and the film itself. He is really a master of all the tools of his trade."6 In other words, without detracting from Zsigmond, who is also a master, or Jean Bofferty, the fine cinematographer on Thieves, the fact that the visual beauty of Thieves Like Us is particularly reminiscent of McCabe and Mrs. Miller would seem to indicate that Altman is the individual most responsible for the consistent look of his films.

Similarly, with regard to sound, not only the repeated use of overlapping dialogue, but the entire auditory strategy of all his films points toward Altman as their main controlling intelligence. In Thieves Like Us, Altman's soundtrack is particularly notable for its absence of background music of any kind. In its place, however, Altman relies heavily on a series of radio dramas that often comment on the action. Far and away the film's most conspicuous device, the use of these broadcasts provides us with a prime example of the way Altman seeks to create a bisociative undercurrent of

tension, in lieu of traditional dramatic conflict.   That is to
say that, like so many of his films, Thieves Like Us depends on a clash of styles (realistic and antirealistic) to
achieve thematic resonance than it does on the more typical
generic clash--in this case, of cops and robbers.

Thieves's episodic story begins in the midst of a
prison break.   Opening with an image of an empty Mississip-
pi field, Altman's highly mobile camera proceeds to track a
prison vehicle before pulling back to reveal two men in a
boat.   Some, mostly unintelligible because of overlapping,
dialogue ensues, in which one of the two men makes a reference (not uncommon in Altman's films) to marijuana.   As
the men from the boat meet the car, Altman zooms in to a
three-shot while one of them, Chicamaw (John Schuck) pulls
a gun on the driver, Jasbo.   Now T-Dub (Bert Remsen)
emerges from the back of the car and the escapees (Bowie
is the other man) begin to change out of their prison clothes.
As the credits begin, they drive off amidst a barrage of
overlapping dialogue, which has the thieves comically ridi-
culing Jasbo.

By playing this first sequence largely for laughs, Altman establishes a deceptively light tone, which further differentiates Thieves Like Us from other films of this genre.
This tone is carried over to the next scene, in which the
three thieves, in their long-johns, are holed up in a barn.
Only now, Bowie's separateness is indicated by his silence
while T-Dub and Chicamaw joyfully reminisce about their
bankrobbing exploits.   After the three are forced to split up,
Altman adds to this sense of Bowie's youthful isolation by
cutting to a shot of him while he waits, for one of the other
thieves to pick him up, alone under some railroad tracks.
When a stray dog approaches, Bowie innocently asks him,
"You belong to someone or are you just a thief like me?,"
before curling up with the dog for protection against the cold.

The next day, Bowie meets up with Chicamaw and
T-Dub at Dee (Tom Skerritt) Mobley's ramshackle service
station.   It is here that Bowie meets Keechie, and the two
young people begin to fall in love.   On the porch, with his
baseball glove in hand, Bowie drinks a Coke and listens to
the radio, in contrast to his two older sidekicks, who drink
whiskey and check out their coverage in the press.   Like
the radio, the newspaper is another communications medium
that serves as one of Altman's motifs.   Moreover, it is
from the newspaper that Chicamaw and T-Dub (and the audi-

ence) first learn that Bowie had been serving a life sentence
for murder since the age of sixteen.  Unlike Bowie, Chicamaw and T-Dub are continually obsessed with the false sense
of importance that their clippings give them.  However, the
humorous manner in which Altman handles their reactions to
their notoriety in these early sequences tends to obfuscate
the ramifications of their self-delusions.

Meanwhile, Bowie begins to woo Keechie with a series of lighthearted jokes ("Do you know what the Mississip-
pi state animal is?  A squashed dog on the road"), which
also distracts us from the more serious implications of his
plight.  Shot mostly in soft, muted tones, the couple's
courtship is marked by their tender naivete, neither of them
having been involved in a mature relationship before.  Here
again, Altman's almost casual visual style (in contrast to
that of most films noirs) is "open" in the sense that it does
not initially attempt to portray the thieves' world as a highly
enclosed web of darkness from which there can be no escape.
Using a variety of medium and long shots, Altman gives his
characters room to breathe.  Consequently, when he does
undercut their misplaced feelings of security, it is often
quite difficult to know how we are meant to react.  A good
example of this occurs when Altman returns to his use of
animal references by having Keechie inform Bowie that his
dog has run off, and the young man replies, "It's all right,
wasn't my dog anyway."

This sense of distance also characterizes Altman's
treatment of the thieves' first on-screen robbery.  Relying
once more on ironic humor as opposed to action, Altman
prefaces this scene with T-Dub's remark that this will be
his thirtieth bank.  After this, the men draw straws to see
who will remain on the outside with the car.  T-Dub picks
the short straw, but, because he has a bad leg that prevents
him from driving, they pick again.  When T-Dub draws the
same straw once more, however, the men realize that Bowie
can't rob a bank anyway, so he'll have to drive.  The robbery itself isn't even shown, as Altman only follows T-Dub
and Chicamaw to the bank door (zoom-in), preferring to di-
vert our attention to the Gangbusters excerpt that emanates
from the car radio.  Typical of the film's early emphasis
on male camaraderie, the scene ends as the threesome
drive off, laughing.

The thieves' next bank job follows the same pattern,
only this time Chicamaw waits in the car.  Steve Gibson of

the <u>International Secret Police</u> is on the radio while T-Dub
and Bowie do the inside work.  Altman also adds another
ironic touch to the scene in the form of a giant Coca-Cola
bottle that is evidently a part of a local promotion for the
beverage.   Linking advertising to both the radio and the
print media's ever-expanding sphere of influence, Altman's
use of ironic period details like this is one of the major
ways in which he "documents" the changes that were taking
place in America at that time.   Simultaneously, the media's
function as an integral part of the narrative is exemplified
by the way that Altman cuts from the bank job to a moving
shot, in Mattie's house, which reveals T-Dub listening to
the radio for news of their hold-up.

     In the ensuing scenes, although Mattie's authoritarian
middle-class ways (she is T-Dub's cousin) contrast sharply
with the behavior of the thieves, Altman maintains his distance by declining to take sides.   Moreover, it is this balanced treatment of both "realists" and "dreamers" alike that
distances our own reaction and pervades <u>Thieves Like Us</u>
with an unexpected feeling of openness.   Despite the obvious
irony of Mattie's sternness with her children while she does
her best to make the three escaped criminals feel at home,
her staunch manner ensures her at least a cool measure of
our respect.   A good example of how this is achieved involves that hilarious scene in which T-Dub and Chicamaw
act out their "36th. "  Using Lula (Ann Latham) and Mattie's
young boy, Joey, as their straight men, this drunken cha-
rade is highlighted by T-Dub's comical insistence that the
reluctant Lula play alone (he keeps telling her that "this is
a <u>real</u> gun").   Finally, Mattie ends their game because it's
time for Joey to do the dishes.

     Deciding to split up for a month before pulling off
their next robbery, Chicamaw and Bowie head up toward
Hermanville, where Altman will concentrate on the expanding relationship between Bowie and Keechie.   Before they
leave, however, Altman inserts what turns out to be the
threesome's last untainted demonstration of their comrade-
ship.   As usual, though, this scene is strewn with irony,
as T-Dub's joyous proclamation that "there'll never be three
like us again" is followed by his fatherly admission to Bowie
that he should have been a doctor or a lawyer ('I could've
robbed people with my brain").   At the same time, the futility of Bowie's situation is subtly indicated by his use of
the past tense when he replies that the only thing he "could've"
done was pitch baseball.

The radical change in mood that characterizes the re-
mainder of Thieves Like Us is the result of two central factors.   The first is provoked by the automobile accident that
Bowie gets involved in while driving to Hermanville.   As a
consequence of this, Chicamaw is forced to kill two lawmen
in order to facilitate their escape.   In this instance, as opposed to the prior bank robberies, Altman's camera is there
to record the violence of the crime, a fact that adds im-
measurable impact to the inherent gravity of the deed.   The
second factor hinges on the effect that the growing relationship between Bowie and Keechie has on all concerned.   This
factor, although somewhat less tangible than the first, requires a great deal more development.

After Chicamaw drops the injured Bowie off at Dee's,
Altman switches focus from the growing bond between the
men to a type of love and companionship that Bowie has
never known.   Here, Keechie nurses him back to health,
and before long the young couple find themselves enmeshed
in a joyful round of love-making.   Along with the slew of
evocative posters that cover the walls, these scenes are also
marked by the film's most overt device as Altman uses the
omnipresent radio to comment upon the action.   More specifically, their romantic union is prefaced by the following
line from the radio's vulgarization of Romeo and Juliet:
"Thus did Romeo and Juliet consummate their first interview
by falling madly in love with each other."   Moments later,
as they renew their efforts, this line is repeated again, and
then a third time.   Consequently, although this sequence
emphasizes their tender naivete, Altman actually succeeds
in undercutting the poignancy of their relationship through
the use of this conspicuously repetitious device.

And it is precisely its conspicuousness that is at issue, as the radio virtually intercedes for Altman's antiromantic persona by transferring our attention from the illusion
of love to the filmmaker himself.   Moreover, the very bold-
ness of Altman's modernist assertion is remarkably consistent with the film's overall strategy of deflating his characters' illusions.   Repetition, in this case, is not just an intuitive flaunting of the filmmaker's ego, but a clever way of
reminding the viewer that love can be a potent source of de-
lusion.   Similarly, by contrasting the thieves' aimless actions with the many glorified myths perpetrated by the media
(Gangbusters, Heart of Gold, Steve Gibson, The Shadow,
etc.), Altman points out the absurdity of their existence.

Another way in which Altman undercuts Bowie and Keechie's relationship is by following their love-making with Bowie's false confession that he killed two "laws" on the way to Hermanville.  Although Keechie intuitively knows that it wasn't Bowie who did the killing, his willingness to take the blame is tantamount to an expression of loyalty that favors the thieves over Keechie.  In conjunction with this confession, a major change in Bowie's character is brought out by his subsequent comment that he's "not sorry."  To which he adds that his only regret is that he didn't get a hundred thousand dollars--he got nineteen--or the chance to pitch pro ball.  However, the couple still entertain the hope that they may someday be able to settle down in Mexico, a fantasy that Bowie's increasing involvement with the thieves would seem to negate.  Thus, when he refuses to promise Keechie that he will quit working with T-Dub and Chicamaw, Bowie actually seals his own fate.  Additionally, after T-Dub runs down their next job, Bowie's blunt enthusiasm about the money he hopes to make serves to distance him even further from both Keechie and the audience.

Thieves's change of tone is also reflected in the way that Altman handles the thieves' next heist.  Whereas their previous robberies were all shot from outside the banks, Altman now moves his camera inside and covers their actions in much greater detail.  Furthermore, that detail now includes Chicamaw and T-Dub murdering a banker as the trio make their getaway.  The next shot is a bravura effort that sums up the extent to which things have changed.  Following a dissolve from the bank, the camera slowly pans across an empty room before coming to rest upon the threesome, who are seated at a table.  The mood is tense. T-Dub wants them both to go with him to pick up Lula, but Bowie is intent on getting back to Keechie.  After Chicamaw tells Bowie that he's "getting pretty stuck up for a country boy," Chicamaw and T-Dub leave while the camera lingers on Bowie, who has graduated from Coke to whiskey.

Realizing that his actions have put an end to their hope, Keechie also threatens to leave Bowie, just after her lover has heard (on the radio) that T-Dub has been shot and Chicamaw is on his way to jail.  Because Keechie also realizes that her inexperience and gawky looks leave her with no alternative, she relents.  This is revealed in a telling zoom-in to Keechie as she examines herself in the mirror (her reflection is distorted).  Now Keechie's assessment, that Bowie chose the thieves instead of her, is confirmed

with another zoom-in to Bowie, as he bids T-Dub good night
in front of the fire.

On the run again, Bowie takes Keechie to The Grapes
Motor Hotel, which T-Dub had previously bought for Mattie.
However, since T-Dub is now dead, Mattie doesn't want anything more to do with the couple.   It is only after Bowie
threatens her that she, ever the realist, agrees to put them
up.    From here, Bowie leaves Keechie in order to spring
Chicamaw from prison.    Although his daring plan of escape
is successful, this, too, is undercut as Chicamaw has become so psychotic that Bowie is forced to turn him out on
the road.    Returning to the hotel, the film reaches its climax when Bowie is gunned down by a group of state troopers who have been alerted by Mattie.

In the novel, both Keechie and Bowie die at the end
(cf. the ending of Bonnie and Clyde).    They Live by Night,
on the other hand, concludes with a more traditionally romantic scene as Keechie reads Bowie's note to her out loud,
turning toward the camera, in an extreme close-up, when
she gets to the final line--"I love you."   Altman's version,
however, is devoid of any such notion of redemption through
romantic love.    For, instead of using Bowie's death to trig-
ger an emotional reaction on the part of the viewer, Thieves
Like Us makes a much more open, and distanced, statement
about survival.    Thus, as she and Mattie witness Bowie's
death, Altman uses slow-motion on Keechie's reaction to
emphasize Keechie's personal sense of agony and loss.
Moreover, by having the police shoot at Bowie through the
walls of his cottage, Altman ensures that most of our attention will be focused on her and Mattie (the "survivors"),
as Mattie holds Keechie back once the shooting starts.

Following this, Altman tacks on a brief epilogue that
serves to deflate any intimations of romanticism the previous
scenes may have contained.    This is accomplished by cutting
directly to a railroad station (zoom-out from a radio) where
Keechie is seemingly prepared to board whatever train is
leaving next.   Ironically, the radio is broadcasting a sermon
on the virtues of the American way.    Then, after lying to a
fellow passenger (Joan Tewkesbury) about the cause of Bowie's
death, Keechie displays her ultimate lack of illusion by adding that she's not going to name her soon-to-be-born child
after its father.    According to Tewkesbury (also the cowriter
of Thieves), "Altman felt very strongly that if you wanted to
make a statement at all, it was that that kind of lady sur-

vived, that the Matties survived, that the Keechies survived. Keechie turned into Mattie. The boys got shot down, but that kind of hard, embittered woman survived and sired a lot of us. "7  Finally, it is the isolated quality of Keechie's survival that Altman chooses to end with, as Keechie's disappearance up the stairway to the platform is followed by a slow-motion long shot in which the other passengers move out of frame, leaving us with the lonely image of an empty staircase.

## The Long Goodbye (1973)

Nothing is more indicative of the bisociative complexity of Altman's films than the incredibly diverse criticisms that they engender. Thus, while Nashville and The Long Goodbye both made The New York Times' ten-best list, the former has been assailed by Gene Youngblood, and the latter by Kenneth Turan, as among the worst films of all time. In the case of The Long Goodbye, most of its detractors have indicated their displeasure with the way that Altman and screenwriter Leigh Brackett have taken liberties with the Raymond Chandler novel that serves as its source. As Brackett has said, "In its first release, the film was greeted, by some critics, with the tone of outrage generally reserved for those who tamper with the Bible. "8  Meanwhile, Altman himself may have put his finger on a more deep-rooted cause of audience resentment when he stated that "audiences are disturbed because it raises questions about their own moral hypocrisy. "9

In any event, Altman's comment does clue us in to many of his major intentions vis-à-vis The Long Goodbye. That is, the film is a virtual three-pronged plan that is aimed at revealing the illusions of its character, or those created by its character, the very form within which they function, and the audience itself. Like McCabe and Mrs. Miller and Thieves Like Us, The Long Goodbye traces its protagonist's increasing loss of control within an overall structure that gains resonance through its generic affiliations. At the same time, however, The Long Goodbye subverts our expectations from the genre (and from Altman's "typical auteurist structure") to a greater degree than either of these other two films. Moreover, by giving the film a contemporary setting, Altman goes one step beyond McCabe

and Thieves in providing the viewer with an updated account
of the way he sees things in the seventies.

If we use Buffalo Bill and the Indians as another
point of reference, the bisociative beauty of The Long Goodbye can be further defined in terms of its openness.   Despite their illusions, viewers are still encouraged to identify
with Altman's Marlowe in a way that the open-and-shut case
of Buffalo Bill would never allow.   Whereas Buffalo Bill's
thematic thrust depends on the filmmaker's unequivocal deflation of the myths surrounding its protagonist, The Long
Goodbye rejects this notion of closure by infusing the film
with a sense of ambiguity and moral uncertainty (on various
structural levels) that undermines the viewer's own feelings
of certitude.   In other words, as Robin Wood has said, uncertainty "has become part of the method and the texture of
the film as well as its subject matter. "10

As mentioned, genre aids in this process by providing
the filmmakers with an arsenal of preconceived codes and
conventions that can then be manipulated to achieve the de-
sired effect.   For example, the hardboiled detective, as conceived by Chandler and Dashiell Hammett, is a fiercely independent sort whose pride and personal integrity are more
important to him than material success.   Thus, although
Chandler himself saw him as somewhat of a pawn and a
"loser, " Marlowe's honorable (and ultimately efficient) practice of his profession more than compensated for his trouble
and lack of worldly riches.   On the other hand, Altman's
conception of Marlowe is intent on stripping away the illusions fostered by these generic conventions, without actually
stepping outside the genre itself (cf. Buffalo Bill).   As he
has stated, "I see Marlowe the way that Chandler saw him,
a loser.   But a real loser, not the fake winner that Chandler made out of him.   A loser all the way. "11

On the surface, Altman's Marlowe comes off as a
loser due to his inability to adjust to the times.   He wears
an old-fashioned suit, smokes nonfiltered cigarettes, and
drives a 1940s sedan.   But Marlowe's problems run far
deeper than this, for Altman's point is not merely that the
moral code symbolized by Marlowe's antiquated lifestyle is
out of date, but rather that its successful application in real
life was never anything more than a carefully constructed
illusion.   By the same token, when Altman arms a contemporary counterculture hero (Elliott Gould) and gives him a
license to kill, the director undercuts one set of illusions

From The Long Goodbye

only to replace them with another.  The central paradox of
this observation is that if The Long Goodbye makes any statement at all, it is that if we (the viewer, the artist, and the
characters) put our faith in illusions rather than reality, we
will always come out as losers.

Put another way, Altman replaces one set of traditional illusions with an attitude epitomized by Gould's repeated refrain, "It's all right by me"--which is emblematic
of the equally potent illusion of the outsider's control of his
or her own destiny.  In spite of the many ways in which
Gould's Marlowe is cut down, he still manages to maintain
a relatively positive grip on the viewer's sympathies.  In
fact, it is the way that Altman overtly manipulates our
reactions--not only to Marlowe, but to the entire spectacle--
that imbues The Long Goodbye with its aura of ambiguity and
uncertainty.  As opposed to the traditional Hollywood window
to the world, in which nothing overtly intervenes between the
spectator and the action, "The Long Goodbye is 'a film by
Robert Altman'--we cannot escape the director's omnipresent
consciousness.  The implicit statement is no longer 'This is
the way things happen,' but 'This is how I see the world.' "12

Consequently, among all of Altman's films, The Long
Goodbye most clearly exemplifies the fact that illusionism and
self-reflexivity are not mutually exclusive.  What adds to the
complexity of this assessment is that Altman "sees the
world" as immersed in an endless struggle between illusion
and reality.  This is best illustrated by the way that Altman
suspends Marlowe between the real world of Los Angeles
and the "dream factory" to which he owes his very existence.
As I've tried to indicate, The Long Goodbye is not just a
comment on the displaced values of its protagonist, but a
calling into question of the false sense of moral justice that
Hollywood has traditionally passed off as "the way things
happen. "

Accordingly, Marlowe's failings stem from the erron-
eous belief that his self-deluded sense of morality will ensure his success à la Chandler's creation.  As Brackett
tells it:

> We did not contravene these [Chandler's] tenets.
> Gould's Marlowe is a man of simple faith, honesty,
> trust, and complete integrity.  All we did was strip
> him of the fake hero attributes.  Chandler's Mar-
> lowe always knew more than the cops.  He could

> be beaten to a pulp, but he always came out on
> top one way or another.  By sheer force of per-
> sonality, professional expertise, and gall, he al-
> ways had an edge.  We said, "A man like this
> hasn't got an edge.  He gets kicked around.  Peo-
> ple don't take him seriously.  They don't know
> what he's all about, and they don't care.  So in-
> stead of being the tough guy, Marlowe became the
> patsy. "13

More specifically, Marlowe's first mistake is not
simply that he jeopardizes his own freedom in order to aid
Terry Lennox (Jim Bouton)--for what else are old friends
for?--but rather it is the blind manner in which Marlowe
caters to Lennox's requests without ever questioning his innocence that tips us off to the fact that he might be a loser.
Then, again, maybe not.  For, up to this point, Altman has
failed to give us enough information to make an accurate
judgment.  Meanwhile, as a result of his efforts, Marlowe
does get kicked around by the police.  As the plot progresses, however, the senselessness of Marlowe's quest seems
to become more of a negative commentary on the devious
"realists" (Lennox, Dr. Verringer, Marty Augustine, Eileen
Wade) who populate The Long Goodbye, than a reflection of
the protagonist's own ineptitude.  Moreover, despite his penchant for wrongheaded assumptions, Marlowe does get things
done.  This is most strikingly revealed at the end of The
Long Goodbye, when Marlowe does, in fact, solve the film's
major mystery.

Yet it is largely because it surrenders the kind of
historical distance that enabled the viewer to interpret
McCabe's and Bowie's actions with some measure of objec-
tivity that The Long Goodbye remains a much more blurry
vision.  In conjunction with this, it is safe to say that there
is inevitably something in many of his major characters that
Altman identifies with--the boyish, adolescent charm of the
lovable loser, and so forth.  Although it has already been
alluded to in passing, in the case of The Long Goodbye this
attitude is particularly difficult to gloss over, for it represents
a way of putting oneself down (cf. "smart-ass" and "cutie-
pie") that thinly disguises one's own feelings of superiority.
(Again I am referring specifically to Marlowe, and to Altman by implication. )

Just as frequently in the director's works, the accompanying vision of this "dreamer" character underlies a

sense of hopelessness and despair that culminates in the
hero's defeat (cf. McCabe and Bowie).   But The Long Goodbye is a far more nihilistic vision than is common for Altman.   The protagonist is permitted to exorcize his illusions
in the ultimate act of retribution--murder--without having to
pay the price that society usually exacts for such deeds.
And yet, the hero's act of anger and revenge (which Altman
seems to share) is only superficially cathartic, because its
targets are too obvious and its intellectual basis is not nearly well enough thought out.   Still, there is another force op-
erative in the film whose integration with these other elements transforms the whole into the kind of modernist experience that goes beyond literal content.   Once again, I am
referring to the force of paradox, or coherent contradiction,
which offers up the potential for the viewer to engage in this
synergistic experience.

     In an effort to come to grips with Altman's use of
paradox in The Long Goodbye, Howard Hawks's The Big
Sleep (also scripted by Brackett from the Chandler novel) in
1946 provides us with another useful comparison.   Equally
obtuse in terms of plot, Hawks's film never leaves us in any
doubt as to how we are to react to Marlowe (Humphrey Bo-
gart).   Consequently, Hawks favored the kind of sparse and
functional ("invisible") style that would correspond to the
clearcut moral climate of his film.   In The Long Goodbye,
on the other hand, Altman's (and cinematographer Vilmos
Zsigmond's) camera is almost continually in motion, and
often appears to have no functional relationship to the action at hand.   Altman's camera does not necessarily locate
or illustrate anything.   It simply moves in the same apparently aimless fashion as the protagonist himself.   Thus, although their styles are quite different, Hawks and Altman
both use them to define the atmosphere in which their characters function. 14

     The most outstanding feature of Altman's visual style
is undoubtedly his use of the zoom.   Together with such other camera movements as pans, tilts, and dollies or tracking
shots, The Long Goodbye uses the zoom as a counterpoint
to its laid-back characters and as a device calculated to
maintain a high level of audience involvement.   This can be
observed during the film's first sequence, which opens with
a pan past an open door to Marlowe, who is lying on his
bed, fully dressed.   After his cat wakens him, Altman
zooms in on Marlowe (without cutting), who opens his eyes,
lights a cigarette butt, and begins to search for some cat

food. Following this zoom, the camera works at cross-purposes to these mundane actions by continuing to move "nervously" around the room, while Marlowe, talking to himself, seasons the cat food with several globs of cottage cheese. [15]

At other times, the zoom is used instead of the straight close-up to emphasize a reaction. Thus, when the lieutenant first informs Marlowe of Sylvia Lennox's death, the camera zooms in on Marlowe. Shortly thereafter, this movement is repeated when the cops tell Marlowe that Terry is also dead, and that the case is now closed. In a similar but far less conventional manner, Altman uses the zoom as a means of building tension. Accordingly, just before that shocking moment when Marty Augustine (Mark Rydell) smashes his girlfriend's face with a Coke bottle, Altman employs a series of zoom-ins to close-ups of the girl's face. But rather than simply following these shots with Augustine's violent act, Altman prefaces his actions with a zoom-out from the girl. That is, by establishing one pattern of movement and then changing it abruptly, Altman's camera style diverts the viewer's attention and imparts added impact to the shockwaves that are about to follow.

Another variation of this technique occurs toward the end of the film when Marlowe finally locates Lennox. After zooming in and out on separate shots of both characters with a minimum of accompanying action, Altman confounds our sense of anticipation by zooming in again, first on Lennox, and then on Marlowe. Then, as Marlowe shoots his nemesis, the camera zooms out once more from a close-up (the end point of the previous zoom) of Marlowe's face. Zooms are also used throughout The Long Goodbye to provide the viewer with an almost subliminal feeling of futility and uncertainty. In conjunction with other camera movements (especially Altman's circular dollies), these zooms appear to build tension where none exists by guiding the viewer to an empty or insignificant point of focus.

In all cases, the zoom-in also distorts our sense of physical reality by flattening the depth of field. Moreover, its cumulative effect serves the self-reflexive purpose of calling our attention to the director's presence. Consequently, another paradox is established, inasmuch as this anti-illusionist stance is arrived at through the use of a device that simultaneously creates its own sense of illusion by manipulating our consciousness and emotions in a variety of ways.

Finally, the zoom's frequent use in connection with glass
surfaces (usually windows in The Long Goodbye) reveals itself as a means of creating ambiguity and uncertainty on
both the physical and metaphorical level.   Not only do these
window shots add an additional plane of action, their accompanying reflections invariably entail still another, less well-
defined, image to be contemplated.   The repeated glimpse of
Marlowe's spaced-out neighbors through his apartment window, his surreptitious observations of Verringer (Henry Gibson), Roger Wade (Sterling Hayden), Augustine, and Eileen
Wade (Nina Van Pallandt), and the "smart-ass and cutie-pie"
sequence in which the cops observe Marlowe through a one-
way mirror are all particularly worthy of mention within the
present context.

Two of The Long Goodbye's most virtuoso visual sequences also make use of windows the further to complicate
the action.   Just before Roger's suicide, for example, we
are distracted from Eileen's answers to Marlowe's questions
(about Roger's relationship to Sylvia Lennox) by a rack focus
on Wade entering the ocean, as seen through the front window of the beach house.   Then Altman cuts to a different
set-up, outside the window, and we see Eileen and Marlowe,
but can no longer hear them.   In an earlier scene, the
beachhouse windows (along with the zoom) are used to undercut our sense of spatial reality, as Marlowe's reflection implicates him in one of the few crucial scenes in which he is
not actually present.   This is accomplished by shooting the
Wades' argument, which is audible to us, from outside their
window, so that Marlowe's reflection (he is outside, facing
the ocean) appears to come between them.   After a series
of close-ups (inside the house), the camera follows Roger as
he leaves to join Marlowe before zooming in on Eileen, who
is seen, as she begins to walk out of frame, through the
window.

The improvisatory performances in The Long Goodbye
function as a sort of corollary to Altman and Zsigmond's
camera movements.   That is, they both add and detract from
the overall sense of filmic reality.   On the one hand, they
are consistent not only with the film's deceptively "off-the-
cuff" cinematography, but with its dominant tone of aimless
uncertainty.   Gould's portrayal in particular is noteworthy
for the way that it uses freewheeling improvisation to mask
a latent sense of vulnerability and hopelessness.   According
to Altman, Gould himself was in a rather depressed state at
the time of shooting, and I think this comes across in the

film just enough to suit the director's double-edged intentions. Moreover, Altman's desire to work with Gould again, after M*A*S*H, is indicative of his strategy of contrasting contemporary attitudes and forms with those of an earlier era. Thus, Gould's off-screen image of the happy-go-lucky neurotic is perfectly suited to Altman's conception of Marlowe as "a loser all the way."

On the other hand, Gould is the kind of modern-day star whose appeal is largely bound up in his antiestablishment persona.   Consequently, his sloppiness and rather eccentric sense of style only serve to heighten the illusions surrounding this "lovable loser."   For, regardless of Altman's stated intentions, it is difficult to see how he strips Marlowe of his "fake hero attributes" after witnessing Gould's performance.   Rather, Altman plays with, almost flaunts, the changing codes of heroic attributes in a way that the motion-picture code of the forties never would have allowed.   My point is that Altman has created a contemporary entertainment that merely substitutes illusionistic elements geared to a sort of "sixties" sensibility for their less sophisticated, because they are more one-dimensional, forties counterparts.   Improvisation is a part of this.   So is the playful type of casting that Altman indulges in.

Among the film's most despicable realists, Lennox (Jim Bouton) is a former baseball star; Verringer (Gibson), a former Laugh-In comic; and Augustine (Mark Rydell) is a working Hollywood director (Cinderella Liberty).   Unlike the stock characters that they portray, however, Eileen Wade (Van Pallandt) is much more difficult to figure out.   Although she is in cahoots with Terry Lennox, she seems to have a genuine concern for her husband, as opposed to the novel, in which she murders him.   Along with Roger, Eileen also has a real capacity for suffering, which further differentiates her from Altman's dehumanized villains.   Sterling Hayden's Roger ("Roger Wade is so close to myself") is the film's true loser.   He is also, with the exception of Marlowe, Altman's most sympathetic character.   His problem is simply that he's too weak to stand up to the illusions, largely his own, and the hypocrisy that he sees right through in his more lucid moments.

In addition to the subtle intimation of self-parody inherent in its casting, The Long Goodbye is loaded with the kind of self-reflexive motifs that tend to elicit bisociative reactions.   The most prominent of these motifs involves the oft-repeated variations of fragments of the title song. Reminiscent of the way that Leonard Cohen's music functioned in McCabe, this use of the soundtrack is considerably more complex due to its omnipresence within the fiction itself. Its self-reflexive implications are hinted at by the only other bit of music employed in the film (a brief version of "Hooray for Hollywood" at the very beginning) and by the overt way in which it crops up in the narrative. A lyrical comment on the characters' failure to maintain stable relationships, "The Long Goodbye" is first heard over the opening credits as Terry Lennox leaves the Malibu Colony. Moments later, a different version is heard while Marlowe arrives at the supermarket (to buy cat food), and still another inside the market itself. In the course of the film, both Augustine and Marlowe sing snatches of it, and the song's first few notes are sounded whenever the Wades' doorbell rings. 16

The Long Goodbye's second major self-reflexive motif revolves around a series of filmic references. The guard at the Colony's gate does impressions of Barbara Stanwyck and Walter Brennan, and the use of the Colony itself evokes a host of less-obvious references to the film industry. In fact, one might have expected that Altman would change Roger Wade from a dried-up commercial writer to a dried-up commercial filmmaker; but this is not the case. Nevertheless, Wade's commercial relationship to his art is indicated as one of the many causes of his breakdown, and, by extension, so is the decadent cultural milieu that serves as the home of many of Hollywood's biggest names. Another particularly interesting Hollywood reference occurs in the hospital when Marlowe tells his fully bandaged roommate ("The Mummy") that "I've seen all your pictures, too." And last but not least, the way in which Marlowe (silently) passes Eileen at the very end recalls the conclusion of The Third Man.

On almost every level, then, The Long Goodbye can be seen to satirize its genre while still remaining very much a part of it. Consequently, Altman's hero--although he is quite different from Chandler's--is nonetheless a hero. Finally, it is the film's skillful use of stylistic paradox that ultimately separates it from other recent examples of generic parody. Aside from embodying what we might term "the Altman touch," it is the director's bisociative use of style, in conjunction with the way that style is integrated into the film's overall narrative structure, that challenges the viewer to achieve a new level of cinematic awareness.

## A Perfect Couple (1979)

To a great extent, many of Altman's films discussed thus far are self-reflexive in the sense that film itself has become its own subject. Of course, these films are not merely movies about movies, but rather works in which various illusionist techniques are brought to the viewer's attention through the revelation of the medium's materiality. With regard to genre, it has been shown that by varying traditional patterns in a manner calculated to subvert audience expectations, the generic form becomes a major object of thought (for example, the detective genre is one of The Long Goodbye's primary subjects). It has also been suggested that such a process can create the potential for certain types of spectator interactions that would not otherwise be possible.

There are, however, different kinds of self-reflexive strategies. Most films (some self-reflexive films) are designed to get the viewer to suspend doubt, to submit to the film as its own reality, which is to be passively consumed. Psychological passivity is not distance, but an empathetic relationship to the film that has traditionally been the dominant mode of cinematic experience. Interaction through distanciation, on the other hand, is one alternative to this mode. Rather than surrendering to the filmic illusion, structures of distanciation (i. e., the rigorous use of certain overt devices) may enable the viewer to maintain a certain sense of autonomy, or separateness from the film. Naturally, many films of this type run the risk that the overly "separated" spectator may bolt and run--or simply never arrive at the theater. But, as Altman's best films attest, there can be a tension between "pleasure" and distanciation that both encourages reflections on the structure of the message and allows for meaningful interactions on the part of the spectator.

A Perfect Couple's major problem is that it falls somewhere in between these two principal modes. It not only lacks the energy, style, and traditional appeals that encourage the willing suspension of disbelief but also the sense of integrated openness or tension referred to above (cf. The Long Goodbye, Thieves Like Us, and McCabe and Mrs. Miller). What results is a rather disappointing combination of elements drawn from two related genres (romantic comedy and the musical). Although Altman attempts to update the codes and conventions of each, he does very little that is new, and, on the whole, fails to provide the audience with

From A Perfect Couple

the kind of qualitative experience that devotees of these genres have traditionally sought.

For example, one of the ways in which Altman and screenwriter Allan (A Wedding) Nicholls try to modernize the usual boy-meets-girl story line is by having Alex (Paul Dooley) and Sheila (Marta Heflin) meet through a videodating service. Although this device would seem to offer the (self-reflexive) potential for Altman's characteristically double-edged commentary on technology and isolation, it is never significantly developed. Even more lamentable is the film's lack of musical achievement. For, unlike Nashville, in which the music is an integral part of Altman's themes and structures, the dozen numbers performed by "Keepin' 'Em Off the Streets," the rock group to which Sheila belongs, begin to seem more and more like a gratuitous exercise in enforced tedium.

In this respect, what Altman and Nicholls, who produced all twelve songs, have done is tantamount to creating a rock musical comedy minus any noteworthy rock attraction. That is, given the amount of time that the group is either seen or heard (nearly half the film), it is reasonable to expect that they will either be of great intrinsic interest, as "noted" performers, or in some way crucial to the narrative structure. In fact, they fulfill neither function, for although Sheila is a (peripheral) member of the group, it is not necessary to innundate the audience in almost an hour of mediocre music to make this point. It is also interesting to note that Altman has spoken of these musical numbers as "punctuation," a concept that calls to mind his use of the P. A. transitions in M*A*S*H. My argument is that punctuation by its very nature should be kept brief. On the other hand, if the numbers are thought to be employed in a more conventional manner, then we must judge them on their own merits.

A Perfect Couple deviates from Altman's typical auteurist structure in a way that severely undercuts the audience's potential for character identification. For these dreamer-losers, Alex and Sheila, are basically uninteresting because they suffer less from self-delusions or dreams (often a positive quality in Altman's films) than they do from an often painfully dull inability to assert their own independence. Additionally, they lack the innate sense of attractiveness or imagination with which Altman usually imbues his lovable losers. Moreover, in view of the fact that relationships in Altman's films are rarely lasting, Alex and Sheila's ultimately

successful union rings false because persistence (his) is
about the only thing they have going for them.  By the same
token, these criticisms could quite possibly be overlooked if
the couple and their surroundings were portrayed in more
realistic terms.  On the contrary, however; Alex's family is
so broadly caricatured, and Sheila is so devoid of motivation
(Alex's attraction to Sheila is also a virtual mystery), that
it quickly becomes clear that realism was not what the filmmakers were after.

Thus, it appears that in failing fully to think out, or
execute, their intentions, Altman and Nicholls have left their
characters in a sort of dramatic limbo without compensating
for this lack of resonance in formal terms.  In fact (with a
few notable exceptions), A Perfect Couple's formal structure--
the more or less conventional use of alternating stories--
actually contributes to audience apathy.  The major problems
here have to do with repetitiveness and predictability.  For
example, after a relatively auspicious opening sequence,
which ends with a rather terse description of Sheila's communal lifestyle, Altman cuts to a zoom of a humorous
glimpse of Alex's family.  So far, so good.  The humor is
derived from having their weird assortment of family members look on, in various states of enforced attentiveness,
while Alex's father (Titos Vandis) goes through the motions
of conducting, to the accompaniment of a classical recording.
But when Alex--who is caught trying to sneak in--is sent to
his room after being rebuked for having possibly (this is not
even confirmed) been out with a woman, something goes
awry.  In view of the amount of independence and persistence
that Alex has already demonstrated in the previous sequence,
it is hard to accept this revelation of the docility of the man,
who is in his late thirties.  Here, too, the problem is not
simply that we don't know how to react to his plight (comically, sympathetically, etc.), but rather that its contrived
nature causes us rapidly to cease to care.  In effect, this
undercuts Altman's potentially bisociative point about the
similarity of the couple's predicaments--they are both under
the domination of an authoritarian figure, the head of the
rock group in Sheila's case--despite their clashing lifestyles.
Without even giving us a chance to become involved in Alex's
problems, Altman opts for another "outrageous" contrast.
This occurs when the two other female members of the group
(Heather MacRae and Tomi-Lee Bradley) inform Sheila that
they are going to have a baby sired by Bobbie (Steven Sharp),
who is gay.  However, this contrast of the group's and
Alex's family's sexual mores fails, precisely because it is

so self-consciously contrived to smack of outrageousness.
Although the comparison itself is intended to be broad, the
group's statements--like their music, unfortunately--are presented in a kind of matter-of-fact manner that severely
strains the audience's notions of credibility.

The bulk of the film follows a similar pattern, with
Altman constantly cutting between roughly parallel scenes of
Alex's family and Sheila's.   Similarly, Alex's sequences are
generally more interesting, although marred by their tendency
toward extreme caricature, than those involving the group's
equally, but not intentionally so, unrealistic round of existence.   Another example of this occurs when Altman cuts
from a shot of Alex telling his sister (Belita Moreno) about
his date, to Alex giving virtually the same rap on a video-
tape.   Cut again to a "Keepin' 'Em Off the Streets" rehearsal, which is interrupted by the group's dictatorial leader,
Ted Neely.   In a reprise of Alex's earlier exit, "Teddy"
proceeds to send Sheila off, and fine her, for having a cold.
Then cut again to Alex's father's place of business, where
Alex works the elevator--the same type of elevator that he
operated in Sheila's loft--and dutifully follows his dad.

Several other of the film's less successful scenes
deserve mention for the way that they muddle variations on
such generic staples as mistaken identity, false resolution,
and ultimate realization.   In the first instance, a scheduling
mix-up and Alex's change of cars results in a protracted,
but noncomic, confusion, as both parties assume that they
have been stood up.   In another scene, Alex sneaks Sheila
off to his room in order to avoid the "freaks" that she lives
with.   Discovering them in bed, his father calls Sheila a
whore, which causes her to storm out, maybe forever,
screaming that they're the "weirdos."   Again, because this
scene is so overdone, because Alex's family members are
such cartoon-like weirdos, it lacks any sense of tension.

Finally, when Alex leaves Sheila and returns home to
find that his sister has died, the melodramatic camera work
and use of heartrending strings on the soundtrack combine
with the family's overly ostentatious mourning to undercut the
import of Alex's decision to go back to Sheila.   Moreover,
since Alex's father disowns him, Alex's decision has really
been made for him.   In spite of Altman and Nicholls's propensity for thematic overkill, however, this scene almost
comes off due to the fact that Belita Moreno's Eleousa is by
far the film's most compelling character.   Unfortunately,

though, her screen time is limited and her function in the
narrative all but obscured by a previous scene.   Earlier in
the film, Alex's father tells him that Eleousa is very sick
and "won't be with us much longer," in such a stylized way
that we simply don't know what to make of it.

The scenes that work best in A Perfect Couple are
almost all based on humorous situations in which neither of
the couple's families are involved.   A particularly auspicious
device is the film's opening use of "the imperfect couple,"
who also pop up at various crucial moments throughout the
narrative.   Thus, A Perfect Couple begins with a zoom-out
and then zoom-in to the imperfect couple at the Hollywood
Bowl.   The humor here is derived from both the overly fas-
tidious manner in which this pair manifest their perfectness,
and from the misleading implication that they are the characters alluded to in the title.   This apprehension is abolished,
however, after Altman pans from the imperfect couple to
Alex and Sheila.   Now, the film's center of focus, although
the imperfect couple can be seen in the foreground at first,
begins to revolve around this second couple, as Alex's every
attempt at making their first date a perfect one is foiled by
the elements.

It is symptomatic of A Perfect Couple's lack of co-
hesiveness that even this first sequence begins to bog down
under the burden of Altman and Nicholls's inability to tem-
porize their sense of comic contrivance.   Another example
of this can be observed in the filmmakers' treatment of
Alex's brief fling with an oversexed client of the videodating
service (Ann Ryerson).   Although this episode contains some
genuinely humorous moments, its impact is ultimately dimin-
ished by the cheap sources of comic invention that it builds
up to.   Accordingly, Alex eventually backs off from this relationship after perusing a host of Ryerson's rather kinky
accoutrements:   rubber gloves, chains, Sex in Prison, etc.

The one notable exception to this pattern involves the
sequence of events that occurs after Alex shows up at
Sheila's, following the couple's scheduling mix-up.   Sheila
is waiting for a new dating service beau (played by Allan
Nicholls), but Alex is determined not to be cast out.   When
Nicholls arrives, the two men begin to fight, whereupon
Sheila closes her eyes and inadvertently slugs Alex with a
poker.   Seeing Alex unconscious on the floor--Sheila has
also passed out-- Nicholls beats a hasty retreat, pausing
briefly to wipe some fingerprints off the poker.   In this

instance, humor is achieved by the unlikely tension generated by juxtaposing elements of slapstick with a real physical threat. Moreover, this effect is sustained in the next scene by contrasting the efforts of a chatty young intern, while he's suturing Alex's wounds, with the couple's own feeble attempts at reconciliation.

In the final accounting, however, A Perfect Couple's flaws far outnumber its successes. For Altman and Nicholls's collaboration has resulted in a film that lacks the innovative vitality and wit that enabled A Wedding to overcome many similar deficiencies. Most importantly, A Perfect Couple replaces A Wedding's motivating premise, the attempt "to explore the foibles of a society," with an uncertainty of purpose that its rigorous structural machinations only serve to compound. Thus, even the brilliant technical quality of the film's sound (i.e., "Keepin' 'Em Off the Street's" numbers are heard exactly as performed) is undercut by both its repetitiveness and its lack of integration within the overall narrative structure of the film. Consequently, A Perfect Couple can be seen to exemplify the danger of relying on isolated, disintegrated filmic elements, be they narrative or technical. For, although such a strategy is capable of providing brief moments of pleasure, it sacrifices the kind of unity that makes the bulk of Altman's oeuvre so intriguing.

Countdown (1968) and Quintet (1979)

Even Countdown, Altman's least personal genre film, points toward the filmmaker's desire to avoid the traditional clichés and conventions of most science-fiction films. However, because Altman had very little control over Countdown and was eventually fired from the project, this film is of only marginal interest in the present context.[17] Moreover, despite the early appearance of such Altmanesque trademarks as the zoom and overlapping dialogue, Countdown rarely rises above Warner Brothers' desire to turn out an inexpensive little cofeature.

In brief, the film's dated story line involves a fictitious series of events leading up to the first manned moon shot (which actually occurred one year later). In terms of genre, what is most interesting here is that Countdown's major deviation from the usual conventions of the science-

From Quintet

fiction film is that its first half concentrates almost exclu-
sively on "the human situation behind such endeavors." Like
so many of his more recent heroes, Altman's chief human,
Lee (James Caan), becomes obsessed with a mission that is
much more dangerous than he cares to admit.   After lift-off
(the "count-down"), however, Altman and his collaborator's
moderately interesting use of various audiovisual techniques
is unequal to the task of elevating their material above its
hackneyed conventions.    Thus, at the end of the film, Altman's own soon-to-be patented formula is reversed as Caan's
bravery, or more likely, stupidity (typically, the filmmakers
hedge their bets), is rewarded by the last-minute discovery
of the shelter that will ensure his survival.

        Quintet, on the other hand, provides us with an il-
luminating example of the director's attempts to breathe new
life into the science-fiction genre.   The key to Altman's ambitions can be located in his use of ambiguous narrative
structures that serve to implicate the spectator in his apoc-
alyptic vision.   Above all else, it is Quintet's refusal to explain itself fully in any terms other than its almost mystical
imagery that differentiates it from most other films of this
genre.

Altman has said that <u>Quintet</u> "deals with the death of
a culture."

> It's set probably in the future; or else in the pres-
> ent in a parallel world. It's as if there were a
> mirror planet to ours--one in which life developed
> in a way similar to ours. It's of no known culture.
> The international cast--with all the different accents
> and mannerisms--was chosen to suggest the weird
> meld in this society, and the sense of rootlessness
> and disorientation. 18

<u>Quintet</u>'s central themes have to do with survival in a world
that is on the verge of extinction. But unlike a great many
science-fiction films that reflect a similar fear of the future,
<u>Quintet</u> fails to provide us with even the slightest clue as to
the circumstances that brought about this situation. Moreover, because its "otherworld" setting is devoid of the tech-
nological trappings that permeate most films belonging to
this genre, <u>Quintet</u> comes off more like a contemporary
morality play than a typical science-fiction epic. As noted
by Andrew Sarris, "There are two metaphors here--'Quintet,'
a game resembling existential backgammon, and the Ice Age,
a state of being that goes beyond the Canadian setting to describe contemporary feelings."19 In fact, the feelings that
it does describe are closer to those expressed in <u>Nashville</u>
than they are to most other end-of-the-world narratives.

Like <u>Nashville</u>, <u>Quintet</u> is a mystery with no outright
solution. If we imagine for a moment that some cataclysmic
event has wiped out society as it was portrayed in that earlier film, it is not hard to see how the characters in <u>Quintet</u>
arrived at their present quandary. That is to say that the
distortion of meaning that pervades Altman's Bicentennial vision is simply reduced to its basic essence in <u>Quintet</u>. Accordingly, many of the characters in the film represent residual behaviors or institutions that are no longer capable of
sustaining the life force. In the face of this impending disaster, Altman has nonetheless created an archetypal hero,
Essex (Paul Newman), whose inner-directed quest for survival symbolizes humanity's greatest hope.

The film begins with a long pan across a barren expanse of snow and ice, which serves to establish its bleak
and somber tone. Eventually, the camera reveals two isolated figures struggling across the frozen landscape. Making their way toward a deserted shelter, the couple pause

briefly as a goose flies overhead.   From their subsequent
dialogue, we learn that Newman and his companion, Vivia
(Brigitte Fossey), are on their way to "the city," which
Vivia has never seen.   Besides the fact that Newman was a
seal hunter who ran out of seals, the only other meaningful
information conveyed in this opening comes when Vivia asks
him why they're going to the city:   "You said there was
nothing for you there before--that's why you left."   And Newman replies, "Maybe there is no city any more."

The credit sequence that follows is equally cryptic.
For no apparent reason other than Altman's fascination with
glass surfaces, it begins with a zoom into a glass chandelier, accompanied by an ominous tinkling on the soundtrack.
Tilting down to a roaring fire (credits begin), the shot continues as the camera moves slowly around a large room
adorned with murals until, having turned full cycle, it returns to the original chandelier.   At this point, a number of
characters prepare to engage in an elaborate board game,
over which Grigor (Fernando Rey) presides.

The ambiguity of this opening is augmented by both
the characters' outlandish costumes, which seem to blend
medieval and Renaissance fashions in a slightly off-kilter
way, and by the hauntingly reminiscent quality of the murals,
which seem to recall some of the more compelling images
from an old Life magazine.   At the same time, our assessment of these nostalgic impressions is mediated over by the
dominance of Altman's, and Jean Boffety's, captivating camera movements.   Once again, the zoom is used here in conjunction with other camera movements--and glass surfaces--
to assert the director's presence and to imbue the scene
with an overwhelming air of uncertainty.   Moreover, in subsequent scenes, this lack of certainty will be pivotally con-
trasted to the hero's sense of purpose.

As Essex and Vivia enter the city, the most striking
images of decay are provided by the packs of dogs who gnaw
hungrily at the many corpses strewn about the place.   Once
the couple make their way to the "Information Center," however, we are afforded a brief look at the past glories of this
dying civilization.   Here, Essex contemplates a series of
sophisticated glass diagrams that revolve, usually counter to
Altman's ever-probing camera movements.   The effects of
these contradictory movements are manifold.   Besides creating a mood of uncertainty, this strategy actually works to
signify various meanings that may either be consciously

readable or unconsciously absorbed.   That is, the spectator
is virtually inscribed in the film through its dominant patterns of movement, which are neither arbitrary nor nonin-
volved.

Thematically, the repeated use of this technique in
conjunction with various other filmic elements can be interpreted in terms of the filmmaker's obsession with the nature
of change.   Meanwhile, this very preoccupation is presented
in the form of Quintet's central riddle.   On one level, this
riddle is concerned with the cyclical process of history, an
assumption that is underscored by both the primitive (medieval) appearance of the city and its inhabitants, and the film's
many circular camera movements, while a second level extends within a hypothetical historical period to examine the
struggle between an isolated individual and the existing establishment.   So it is that the reading of Altman's camera
movements, as a corollary to Essex's reading of the revolv-
ing glass diagrams, provides us with an entry point into
Altman's convoluted narrative.

The society depicted in Quintet is plagued by apathy.
The Information Center is empty and unused.   Even Vivia is
nonplussed by Essex's search (he's looking for his brother),
failing to comprehend how five digits and a color code can
help him in his undertaking.   Similarly, when they do manage to locate his brother, Francha (Tom Hill), Essex's enthusiasm about the center is undercut by Francha's lack of
concern for anything but quintet.   Accordingly, Essex is sur-
prised to learn that they still have tournaments "on all levels, " and that the playing of quintet has replaced work for
the majority of the population.   The strangeness of this situation is also compounded by Francha's family's reaction to
Vivia (Francha says she's the youngest person he's seen in
years), inasmuch as they are all flabbergasted that she's
pregnant.

The action resumes with a game of quintet (which is
never fully explained), while Essex, obviously uninterested
in playing, goes out to get some wood.   After we hear
snatches of gaming terms (i. e. , "sixth man, " "limbo, "
"killing order, " etc. ), a black-clad figure, Redstone, rolls
a bomb into Francha's hovel, while Essex talks to the wood
seller.   Running back to Francha's, Essex encounters the
same man in black, just before he views the carnage.   In
this scene, Altman's moving camera functions in a slightly
different manner than it did previously, as the director uses

the zoom to link Essex's point of view with the viewer's. Thus, after a weird electronic musical build-up, Essex sees (via the zoom) Redstone through the window, and takes off after him. Following this, the villain is slain by another unidentified character, and Essex manages to retrieve the dead man's quintet pieces and a list of names.

Back at the hovel, the dogs have already begun to eat the corpses. Then, in a brilliantly orchestrated series of shots, Altman captures the poignant beauty of Essex's devotional act, as Essex begins to remove Vivia's body from the premises. Shot from a high angle, Altman's moving camera continues to follow Essex past the outskirts of the city to the edge of the ice. Here, he gently rolls his lover's body into the water, and looks on as the camera moves with her slowly floating form until it finally submerges. Furthermore, the achievement of this scene is augmented by cutting directly to a shot of Essex in the Information Center. This is Essex's undaunted sense of purpose, his quest for information or knowledge, immediately reaffirmed, despite his many trials and tribulations.

In the Center, another major theme is introduced after Essex's meditations are interrupted by Redstone's killer, St. Christopher (Vittorio Gassman), who queries him. When Essex tells him that he's trying to find a "friend," St. Christopher replies that he hasn't heard that word in a long time; he uses "alliance." Soon, Essex decides to impersonate Redstone at the hotel adjacent to the quintet casino. Having known Redstone, Essex's ploy elicits a chuckle from Grigor, who had designated Redstone as a player in an earlier sequence. Grigor tells his associates, with tongue in cheek, that "this is one of the imponderables." Then, picking up on the as-yet-undeveloped theme of friendship and deceptive gamesmanship, Grigor bursts in on Essex, who has taken a room in the hotel. At first, Grigor feigns that he's entered the wrong room, but soon admits that he's been "playing the sixth man" with Essex. Explaining that he's the judge and interpreter of the rules of quintet, Grigor adds that it's hard to judge and not play, and that he's just looking for companionship. Next, the strange sound of chimes rounds out a transition, as Grigor takes his new-found "friend" to the casino. 20  Here, Grigor tells Ambrosia (Bibi Andersson) that Newman is not dangerous, because "he doesn't like to play games." Shortly thereafter, St. Christopher adds to the confusion by asking Grigor, in private, for a ruling on the imposter. His argument is that he's

followed the rules (by killing Redstone at the right time),
and that a "sensitive" player wouldn't do what Redstone did.

Like Grigor's parody of justice, St. Christopher represents the remains of religion in this society.    Accordingly, his strange church services reveal Quintet's ambiguous,
because it is intentionally equivocal, philosophical center to
contain only a distorted "residual" of religion.    More specifically, it preaches a specious metaphysics of passive acceptance, which is then cunningly tied into quintet.    Essex,
on the other hand, is constantly distinguishing himself from
all the other characters through his insistence on searching
for a more meaningful pattern of existence.    Another example of this occurs after Essex and Ambrosia discover Gold-
star's lifeless body; he's been killed by Deuca (Nine Van
Pallandt).    Essex says that the killing is some kind of ritual, to which she replies that "death is arbitrary" and that
he's "trying to find meaning where none exists."    Similarly,
when Essex questions St. Christopher about the list of names
that he has found, St. Christopher tells him that he is dis-
ruptive.    He adds the warning that Essex will never understand the scheme of things until he's a part of it, "at the
exact moment when it will be too late."

In the next scene, Grigor tells Essex that all the elements of life are contained in quintet, and that the game is
the only thing of value.    Then, after a tilt down to a picture
of a goose on the wall, Essex asks Grigor about the "scheme,"
but gets no further reply.    This use of the goose is noteworthy inasmuch as it bears a striking resemblance to the
bird that Essex watched in the opening scenes.    Moreover,
he identifies with it, as another creature on the verge of
extinction.    This connection is underscored by a zoom into
the goose as Essex asks whether the goose knows where he's
going or just flies about.

When Ambrosia finds St. Christopher in Deuca's room
(he has apparently just killed Deuca by sticking a spike through
her head), the self-assertiveness of Altman's visual style
reaches a kind of peak.    This is accomplished by having
Grigor enter the room so that Altman's composition comes
to resemble an inverted equilateral triangle.    Grigor is at
the bottom tip, facing Ambrosia and St. Christopher, who
stand flanking Deuca at the base.    This configuration, which
places Grigor in a position of power--in conjunction with
Grigor's concurrent ruling that Redstone is part of the
scheme because his life is not important outside the game--

adds a touch of clarity to the interrelationships between these characters.  At the same time, the most noticeable aspect of this scene is a result of the seemingly interminable length of time that Deuca, still with the spike stuck through her head, occupies the approximate center of the frame.  By focusing our attention on this rather absurd image of death, Altman elicits a powerfully distracting sense of uneasiness in the audience, which remains unchecked until Ambrosia belatedly covers Deuca with her cloak.

Besides Essex and Vivia, Ambrosia is the only other character in Quintet who possesses any vestige of hope for the future.  Thus, despite her fatalistic exterior, she feels a strong attraction for Essex.  After they spend the night together, his effect on her is exemplified by the fact that she has recaptured the strength to dream.  However, in her waking state, Ambrosia can only comment that Essex's unconcealed hopes are like those of a child, and there are none any more.  Nevertheless, Ambrosia does try to warn Essex that he is St. Christopher's next victim.  But once Essex has disposed of St. Christopher, the fact that she is incapable of changing is confirmed by her subsequent actions:  she moves in on Essex for the kill, only to find that he has anticipated her intentions; he slashes her throat.

The ultimate uncertainty of Quintet's final sequences is emphasized in several ways.  Stylistically, these include a zoom-out from a blurry chandelier to a pan, past a mural of a melancholy Southeast Asian mother and child, to Essex as he calls out to Grigor, "What's the prize?  I won."  This is answered by more of Grigor's sophisms, which reiterate his belief that the game itself is its own reward and that Essex has nothing more to find or learn.  But Essex isn't buying it.  In fact, his decision to go north makes it clear that Essex's resolute search for something more than quintet is the film's one unambiguous motif.  Finally, Quintet's Incredible Shrinking Man ending leaves the question of humanity's survival in a suspended state, as Altman's camera pulls back from the snow and ice while Essex, walking forward, gets smaller and smaller until he dematerializes in the center of the frame.


NOTES


[1]Joseph Campbell, The Hero with a Thousand Faces

(New York: Pantheon, 1961), p. 3.

2Ibid., pp. 257-58.

3"Lights, Action, Camera! He's a Master of Them All," St. Petersburg Times, February 18, 1979, sec. G, p. 1.

4A great deal of credit for McCabe's look is also due to production designer Leon Ericksen, who also collaborated with Altman on That Cold Day, M*A*S*H, Brewster, Images, California Split, Quintet, and A Perfect Couple.

5For a more thorough discussion of specific differences between They Live by Night and Thieves Like Us, see Robert Philip Kolker, "Night to Day," Sight and Sound, Autumn 1974.

6St. Petersburg Times, sec. G, p. 1.

7Joan Tewkesbury, "Dialogue on Film," American Film, March 1979, p. 45.

8Leigh Brackett, "From 'The Big Sleep' to 'The Long Goodbye' and More or Less How We Got There," Take One 4, p. 28.

9Robert Altman, quoted in Judith M. Kass, Robert Altman: American Innovator (New York: Popular Library, 1978), p. 143.

10Robin Wood, "Smart-ass & Cutie-pie: Notes Toward an Evaluation of Robert Altman," Movie 21, Autumn 1975, p. 10.

11Brackett, "'The Big Sleep' to 'The Long Goodbye,'" p. 28.

12Wood, "Smart-ass & Cutie-pie," p. 8.

13Brackett, "'The Big Sleep' to 'The Long Goodbye,'" p. 28.

14Michael Tarrantino, "Movement as Metaphor: 'The Long Goodbye,'" Sight and Sound, Spring 1975, p. 98. According to Tarrantino, there are no more than twenty static shots in the entire film.

15This is ironic inasmuch as these actions and Marlowe's subsequent attempts to fool his cat by switching cat food cans are Marlowe's most devious maneuvers.

16For a detailed discussion of Altman's use of this musical motif, see Jonathan Rosenbaum, "Improvisation and Interactions in Altmanville," Sight and Sound, Spring 1975.

17See block quote from footnote 8, "Introduction: The Films of Robert Altman," p. 13.

18An untitled interview in Film Comment, September-October 1978, p. 17.

19Andrew Sarris, "Altman at Armageddon," Village Voice, February 19, 1979, p. 45.

20At this point, it should be mentioned that the special sound effects that contribute to Quintet's mood of eerie uncertainty were first used in a similar manner in <u>Three Women</u> (1977), and that credit for their effectiveness must be shared between David Horton, who is credited for "special sound effects" on <u>Quintet</u> and as a "cosound editor" on <u>Three Women</u>, and Richard Portman, who has served as "rerecording mixer" on every Altman film since <u>Nashville</u>, Altman's first Dolby film.

# CHAPTER IV

## FILMS AND DREAMS


Each day art further diminishes its self-respect by
bowing down before external reality; each day the
painter becomes more and more given to painting
not what he dreams but what he sees. Nevertheless, it is a happiness to dream, and it used to
be a glory to express what one dreamt. But I ask
you: does the painter still know this happiness? --
Charles Baudelaire

A film is not a dream that is told but one that we
all dream together -- Jean Cocteau

In most cases, early psychological approaches to film
were based upon a Freudian model that compared the dreamlike aspect of the cinematic experience to the unconscious.
Accordingly, the analyst became a sort of detective who
searched for clues (symbols) that would help to explain the
text. More often than not, this led to a passive attitude
toward the medium, because the examination of symbols as
a disguised representation of a repressed wish, of both the
protagonist and the creator, emphasizes plot patterns and
the text as signified. In other words, this process of de-
coding treated the work as something to be discussed apart
from the spectator. After 1963, however, certain French
theorists, such as Christian Metz and Jacques Lacan, re-
vamped the older Freudian model by emphasizing the relationship between the spectator and the text. Consequently,
the text was now to be treated as a signifier, and the analyst's job was no longer to solve the riddle of the text, but
rather to look for clues that would "open" the situation even
further.

As early as 1916, Hugo Munsterberg's The Photoplay:
A Psychological Study attempted to establish a considerably
different approach to film psychology that is well worth con-

119

sidering in the present context.   Anticipating the findings of
Gestalt psychology, Munsterberg reasoned that every experience can be analyzed in terms of the relationship between a
part and the whole.   He asserted that our perception of
movement in films depends more on the spectator's active
interpretation of a series of still images than upon the static phenomenon of persistence of vision; this active process
later came to be known as "the phi-phenomenon."   Anticipating Cocteau's statement as well, Munsterberg went on to develop a theory of film process in which the spectator was
seen as an active accomplice for the filmmaker.   Finally,
Munsterberg came very close to predicting Altman's own
sentiments when he said, "To picture emotions must be the
central aim of the photoplay. "

     Unlike Munsterberg, whose pre-Freudian approach to
the psychology of film did not lead him to a discussion of
dreams, most popular film theorists make use of some aspect of the dream analogy.   On one level, these comparisons
invariably point to the immediate similarities between the
experience of viewing films and dreaming.   In addition to
our passive position in the darkened theater, most of these
comparisons emphasize film's ability to manipulate space
and time in a manner that closely approximates dreaming.
Films (and dreams) free us from the bounds of the spatial-
temporal continuum that rules our waking state.   Both media
also afford us a sense of being involved in an experience
that we can neither control nor affect, as well as providing
us with a secondary awareness of our separateness from
that experience.

     On a more general (sociological) level, such critics
as Parker Tyler, in the 1940s, wrote about Hollywood as
the source of "daylight dreams" that mirrored mythical cultural values and gave the public a chance to escape their
normal inhibitions.   From this point of view, various national cinemas could be interpreted in terms of manifestations
of a sort of collective unconscious (cf. Siegfried Kracauer's
From Caligari to Hitler).   At the same time, Tyler's elit-
ism also seemed to hint that a truly great film artist could
virtually reprogram the dreams of a society by creating
interactive works of sufficient imaginative power.   But even
for Tyler, this would not be accomplished solely because
film is basically a dream mode (in fact, Tyler argues ve-
hemently that it is not), but rather because film has the potential to represent a level of "psychic consciousness, " em-
bodied by what he terms the "totality" of the film, which can
influence our most deeply rooted thoughts and emotions.

In addition to the subversion of generic codes and conventions, Altman's modernist tendencies have been shown to reside in his use of various bisociative themes and structures. Among these, the director's use of dream structures is particularly revealing. That is to say that, like Baudelaire, Altman sees the subjective realm of dreams as providing fuel for the artist's quest to express the totality of feelings that comprise the experience of reality. Thus, although dream structures are totally dominant in only one of Altman's works (Three Women), he has also directed a large number of films in which the kind of subjectivity that we associate with dreams is manifested by both the filmmaker and his characters. On the technical level, this has been observed in regard to the abrupt spatial-temporal transitions that mark his rather unconventional "linear sequences." In terms of themes, we have only to point to the recurrent figure of the "dreamer" who cuts her- or himself off from reality, in order to make this connection.

It is especially worth reiterating the importance of dreams in relationship to the themes and structures of both Buffalo Bill and Quintet. Altman's subjective use of color is another noteworthy strategy that helped to imbue his period pieces (McCabe and Thieves) with a highly evocative dreamlike quality. Finally, the very "openness" of Altman's narrative structures serves to blur distinctions between fantasy and reality (most notably in The Long Goodbye and Nashville) which are implicit in the works of more traditional filmmakers. In a similar vein, the four films that are about to be discussed (That Cold Day in the Park, Brewster McCloud, Images, and Three Women) merit consideration in terms of dream modes because the blurring of such distinctions has become their dominant structural motif. Interestingly enough, each of these films also concerns itself with sex and death, and, despite stylistic differences among the films, we are almost constantly aware of Altman's self-assertive presence in all four.

In "The Art of Dreaming in Three Women and Providence: Structures of the Self," Marsha Kinder writes that the directors of these two films, Altman and Alain Resnais, "are both reaffirming the self and human creativity on three levels of experience--dreams, conscious artistry, and social interaction."[1] In brief, her provocative argument is that the current onslaught of structuralist thinkers (i. e. , Lacan, Foucault, and Lévi-Strauss) have turned their backs on ego-centered psychologies, which include the "old" Freud, in favor of "Freud's arguments for unconscious structures controlling human behavior, which undermines the illusion of personal freedom. "[2]   Partially in response to this shift in attitude, Kinder suggests that those auteurs who are interested in reaffirming the existence of the self are doing so by creating films "structured like dreams or myths. "   Although That Cold Day in the Park, Brewster McCloud, and Images are not as completely dominated by dream structures as either Providence or Three Women, it is still worth reflecting upon them in terms of Kinder's basic approach:

> Both films lend themselves to a Gestalt approach to dreams in which all characters, settings, and props are seen as projections of the dreamer or aspects of the auteur's personality.   The auteur can be interpreted on several levels. . . .   On a self-reflexive level of aesthetics, Altman, Resnais, and Mercer [who wrote Providence] are the creators, who allude to their own earlier works through casting or allusions and who use their characters, settings, and events to project themselves into the conscious and unconscious minds of their viewers.[3]

One further note of amplification is necessary before proceeding to an analysis of Altman's "dream films. "   Thus far, I have not attempted to psychoanalyze Robert Altman, nor do I intend to begin to do so now.   Although there is no doubt that powerful patterns of his personality are revealed in his films, I am most concerned with the interactive patterns of meaning that are extended to the spectator in various ways.   In other words, while I have tried not to ignore the ramifications of certain recurrent indicators of personality, I am more interested in the ("opening") goal of showing how signification in Altman's films can occur than I am in the ("closing") process of explaining what is signified.   Moreover, we can never fully understand the personality of the artist from his or her work alone, although we can, I believe, extend the boundaries of our own selves by attempting to achieve conscious perception of certain artists' forms.


That Cold Day in the Park (1969)


As previously mentioned, Altman considers That Cold Day in the Park to be his first fully realized feature-length project.   Released in the same year as M*A*S*H, it is a

From That Cold Day in the Park

relatively "small" film, but one that nonetheless reveals
many of the director's formative tendencies.   Among the
most important of these tendencies is his modernist predis-
position to eschew traditional patterns of narrative development and style in favor of the kind of structural ambiguity
that encourages the spectator to play an active role in the
production of meaning.   Similarly, themes of madness in
That Cold Day in the Park express feelings of isolation and
alienation from contemporary society that serve to characterize Altman's early antiestablishment stance.   However,
largely because the film contains no overt social message,
That Cold Day in the Park was attacked by most critics at
the time of its release on the grounds that Altman's stylistic
machinations failed to compensate for the heroine's lack of
motivation and the film's essentially "murky" content.

While it is certainly true that That Cold Day in the
Park is not without its flaws, much of this adverse criticism
seems to stem from a failure to relate to the film in modernist terms.   Of course, it is considerably easier to as-
sess Altman's strategies in retrospect, due to the accumulated distance and evidence of time and his subsequent films.

Yet, it appears to me that such statements as Michael
Dempsey's, "He [Altman] strains to be ornate but cannot relate his devices to his heroine's subjectivity,"[4] misconstrue
an essential aspect of Altman's decoupage in a manner that
is still all too prevalent.   Thus, although I do not intend to
argue that this film is anywhere near a mature masterwork,
I will attempt to clear up some of its accompanying critical
misconceptions.

    In order to do this, it is necessary to refer back to
the Koestlerian notion of logical gaps that the viewer "has to
bridge by his own efforts." In other words, Altman's narrative strategy in That Cold Day in the Park is modernistic in
the sense that it "requires a significant effort from the receiver of the message." This calls for a willing accomplice
who is not only cognizant of the film's narrative elements as
a projection of their auteur, but as the joint product of its
creators, the protagonist, and the viewer.   Accordingly, it
is the oscillations of input amongst this triumvirate that establishes resonance in the film.

    Thus, many of those commentators who criticized
Altman's style for being obvious have failed to take into account the way in which authorial overtness affects the film's
overall narrative strategy.   For example, "refractions from
the windows" do not merely make it clear that Altman's heroine, Frances (Sandy Dennis), is unbalanced (as at least one
critic has observed), but rather they convey impressions of
a nonordinary reality that are shared by the filmmaker and
his protagonist.   To become an active participant in this
process, a viewer must be encouraged to alter his or her
perceptions accordingly.   Consequently, while it can be shown
how Altman attempts to enlist the viewer's participation, it
must be understood that the success of the entire process is
not dependent upon the viewer's willing suspension of disbelief, but rather upon a willingness to cooperate.

    In That Cold Day in the Park, the protagonist's lack
of self-awareness is a major cause of her instability.   Thus,
this film can be viewed as the first of the director's many
attempts to induce an analogous sense of uncertainty in the
spectator.   That is, in working to break up the spectator's
ego structures, Altman, by implication, makes possible the
experience of a nonordinary awareness of the self.   In this
state, dreams and images no longer simply mirror reality
(i. e. , the "reality" that Frances is coming apart), but become an alternative route to internal integration.   And while

the road is fraught with some bumpy going, if one surrenders to the ultimately inexorable rhythm of the journey,
rather than attempt to analyze Frances's "case," a curious
tension is established between Frances's disintegration and
the spectator's own potential to internalize aspects of his or
her splintered psyche.

In That Cold Day in the Park's opening sequences,
structures of ambiguity combine with Altman's use of various
self-assertive techniques to create the dominant mood of the
film.   The main credits, which appear over a series of moving camera shots that follow Frances as she walks home,
end with a zoom-out (just after Altman's credit) from inside
a front window of Frances's flat, as she arrives at the door.
Very shortly, the movement of this first zoom, and the point
of view with which it is associated, is reversed, as Frances
goes to another window and looks out at a young man (Michael Burns) seated on a park bench.   This shot is also accompanied by the same musical motif, from a music box,
that was heard during the opening credit sequence.   Thus,
by inflecting this woman's perceptions with a musical device
that often connotes dream states or other nonordinary modes
of consciousness, Altman immediately calls Frances's mental
state into question.   These intimations are augmented by the
use of repetition (Frances goes back to the window), which
includes several leisurely close-ups of the strangely curious
Frances as she peers out at the boy.

When her dinner guests arrive, however, Frances's
preoccupation with the boy can be seen in another light due
to the stultifying atmosphere of the gathering.   That is, she
seems to look upon it as an escape from her incredibly staid
and boring environment.   Similarly, we are actually encouraged to indulge in her fixation, which continues throughout
the dinner, as an alternative to the drabness of the dinner
proceedings.   In effect, it is these feelings--that anything
would be preferable to the dullness of this group--that sanc-
tion her decision to invite the boy, who's been sitting in the
rain, into her flat.   Likewise, it is the oppressive conserva-
tism of her spinsterish milieu that helps to channel Frances's
(and Altman's and the viewer's) perceptions into a nonordinary realm.

This divergence from everyday reality is immeasur-
ably heightened by the fact that the boy either cannot or will
not talk.   What results is a doubly ambiguous situation, which
is suitably underscored by Altman's constant use of mirrors

and reflecting surfaces. Sometimes these surfaces are integrated into the action, while at other times their utilization
seems to serve a purely formal function. Yet, even a zoom
into a glass bead from a light fixture (a common transition-
ary device in That Cold Day) imbues Altman's content with
meaning due to its accumulated use. Moreover, although
these reflective surfaces and subjective camera movements
often correspond to Frances's psychological state, they are
also Altman's way of manifesting his own subjective presence.

On the narrative level, our first real clue that the
boy may be putting on an act comes when the camera catches
him listening in on Frances's phone conversation. Following
this, the boy makes believe that he's asleep, refusing to respond, even after Frances asks him, "Are you really asleep?"
Curiously enough, this brief interchange tells us a lot about
Frances, inasmuch as her tone seems to indicate that she's
onto his act but nevertheless continues to play her own
little games. In other words, her lack of awareness is
definitely self-oriented, as evinced by her ongoing compulsion
to "explain" even her most trivial thoughts and actions to the
boy, instead of confronting the reality of the moment.

Meanwhile, rather than give us any clear indication of
either character's motives, Altman allows the viewer's imagination to run rampant over his bisociative images. A prime
example of this involves that virtuoso series of shots that
precedes the boy's first nocturnal sojourn. After dissolving
from some glass beads, the camera tilts down and proceeds
to rack-focus as it zooms out through a now discernible
window frame. Then, after another dissolve from the glass
beads, the camera reverses the movement of the previous
zoom and pans to a two-shot of Frances and the boy. She
is explaining that her maid is coming the next day. As she
speaks, the camera continues to move at cross-purposes to
the action, for, after zooming in on the couple (from the
previous two-shot), it simply wanders back to the glass
beads, seemingly impervious--or is it reflective, and, if so,
what of?--to her ramblings. After the two characters say
good night, however, the camera remains static for a few
beats while Frances examines herself in the mirror. Finally, it is the change in rhythm brought about by this static
mirror shot that adds resonance to its metaphoric implications (cf. Frances's apparent schizophrenia).

Following this sequence, the boy leaves her flat via
the bedroom window. It is at this point that Altman partially

reveals the boy's ability to speak, in conjunction with another provocative audiovisual tour de force.   I say "partially," because this initial revelation is so obscured by music and the camera's physical distance from the speaker that a new kind of narrative ambiguity virtually replaces the old.   This feeling of displacement is achieved by following the boy to a house, and then keeping the camera at a great enough distance, outside the house, to permit lingering uncertainty as to what exactly is transpiring inside.   At the same time, the camera's precisely measured movements implicate us in the unfolding of this multifaceted riddle by placing us in the position of a voyeur looking through the windows.   Thus, after the boy enters the house, the camera tilts up one story and stops (we see the boy talk, but his dialogue is muffled) and then repeats this maneuver by tilting up one more level (as the boy moves) before tilting back down.

Shortly thereafter, the boy's role-playing is duly accounted for.   This occurs when Burns relates his recent experiences to his sister (Suzanne Benton) and her boyfriend, and Benton adds that this silent act is something he frequently indulged in as a kid.   As the plot progresses, Altman returns to this new series of interrelationships several times in an apparent attempt to contrast these young people's lifestyles and sexual mores to Frances's.   Using the harsh, garish tones of Vancouver's night life to achieve a formal contrast with the pale, washed-out colors that characterize Frances's environment, these scenes are laden with ambiguous sexual overtones.   On one occasion Benton even manages to sneak up for a bath at Frances's (shades of The Servant), whereupon her initially uneasy brother proceeds to join her in the buff.

On the whole, however, these scenes are neither integrated into the main story, nor do they possess the emotional impact of nearly every scene in which Sandy Dennis is present.   Without Dennis, there is not only a substantial drop-off in acting ability, but an equally crucial absence of the kind of controlling subjectivity that makes Altman's ambiguous narrative structures meaningful.   For example, that curious scene in which the boy shows up at Frances's with what I assume to be some form of hash-cookies would not be anywhere near as effective if Altman and cinematographer Lazlo Kovacs could not play their images off against the dreamlike quality of Frances's doubly stoned-out state.   Accordingly, the shadowy images that accompany the couple's game of blind-man's-bluff do more than make it clear that

the characters are misguided, just as Frances's distorted
reflection in the glass wall does more than signify the quality of her psychic life.    These ostensible metaphors for
madness work to open up meanings rather than enclose them,
much as Frances's little vanity case opens to reveal a mirror that is subsequently included in a wider-angled shot into
yet another, larger mirror.

That Cold Day in the Park's most powerful scene is
notable for the way that it integrates all of Altman's narrative techniques.    After Frances unlocks the boy's door, it
begins with a slow zoom into a back-lit close-up, as Frances
proceeds to bare her soul.    The scene is further subdivided
into two other distinct set-ups that are keyed by Frances's
movements and changes in the way that she is lit.    In the
back-lit section, Frances admits that she is lonely, goes into
a bit of her family background, and finishes by asking if the
boy thinks that she's "old." As she moves into the light,
the mood of her monologue now shifts, as the word "old"
seems to launch her into a scathing attack on her late-
fiftyish doctor-suitor.    In many ways, this is the film's
most ironically revealing passage, as the doctor's brand of
alienated suffering, which so "repulses and disgusts" her,
is, in fact, the very same malady from which she is suffering.    Finally, the third section of the scene, as she
moves to the foot of the bed, in shadow, finds her frustrations seeking a sexual outlet as Frances asks the boy to
make love to her.

In psychoanalytic terms, one might say that at this
point Frances has rejected her father figure in the hope of
transferring her neuroses via her previously repressed sexual drive. [5]    But although her ultimate goal is a healthy one,
her method of seeking integration is compulsively deluded.
Moreover, the effectiveness of this scene is only partially
contingent on its psychological ramifications.    For what imbues it with an almost unbearable degree of tension is the
way that Altman undercuts Frances's most intimate confes-
sions by clouding the entire situation with narrative ambiguity.    From the very beginning of the scene, the viewer is
encouraged to wonder whether or not the boy is actually
present.    Obviously, Frances thinks that he is, but in lieu
of any physical evidence, the viewer is already inclined to
question the accuracy of all of her assumptions.    Consequently, her progressive movements toward the bed build in
an excruciating crescendo, which climaxes when Frances
lifts the blanket off the lump that she presumed to be the

boy--revealing a doll.  As she screams, the camera zooms
in to a close-up of the doll, which she now attacks, before
cutting (by means of traveling focus) to the boy, his sister,
and her boyfriend in a Vancouver nightclub.

Following this, there is a brief lull before the storm.
The boy returns to the flat, and Frances manages to nail up
his windows.  Finding himself a prisoner, the boy utters his
first words to her--a protest--whereupon Frances explains
that she can't let him go, she wants things to remain "as
they are."  Evidently, for Frances, "the way things are"
means that her presumed sexual rejection necessitates the
procurement of a sexual surrogate who will enable her to
retain control over the boy.  Thus, Frances goes out and
picks up a prostitute whom she then locks up in the room
with the boy.

Before I comment on the conclusion of the film, it is
worth reiterating that That Cold Day's major deficiency involves Altman's failure to develop satisfactorily the boy's
role in the narrative.  Unlike the ambiguity that is motivated
by Frances's unstable mental state, the ambiguity surrounding
the boy's motivation is never sufficiently probed or established
to the degree that the viewer might be able to interact with
it.  Instead, we are simply asked to accept the implied explanation that he secretly craves the kind of attention that his
sister lavishes upon her boyfriend.  Or perhaps the situation
is really just one big lark to the boy.  In any event, his enforced union with the prostitute signals the end of the party.
This is presaged by a zoom into an extreme close-up of
Frances as she listens to the sounds of their love-making
from outside the room.  Next, Frances walks out of frame
(the camera remains in a stationary position) and then suddenly reappears as she bursts into the room, leaping on top
of the bed.

At this point, we cannot distinguish one character
from another (due to dim lighting and camera placement),
nor do we know exactly what Frances has in mind.  Even
after the boy jumps up and turns on the light to reveal
Frances and the prostitute, whom she's just stabbed, it is
impossible to know for certain that the prostitute was her
intended victim.  In either case, Frances responds by telling the boy that he doesn't have to be afraid, and that she's
told the woman to go.  During this speech, the familiar musical motif created by the wind chimes and the music box is
quite prominent and continues to rise in volume as the camera

zooms in to an extreme close-up of her kissing him which blurs intermittently as the final credits roll by.

In the end, although sexual frustration has been indicated as a prime cause of Frances's undoing, it is only symptomatic of a larger set of problems. For at no time does Altman advocate repression as a viable solution to Frances's illness, preferring instead to sketch out a subjective sequence of events that merely chronicles his protagonist's disintegration. This, in turn, leads to a basically Laingian notion of society as sick, and schizophrenia as socially induced. Ultimately, however, there is no "right answer" to the film beyond its attempts to implicate the spectator in the highly charged experience of nonordinary reality that it presents.


Brewster McCloud (1970)


Following the international success of M*A*S*H (1969), Altman found himself in the unique position of having more or less free reign on his next feature-length project. Consequently, Brewster McCloud developed into a depository for a flood of heretofore-unused ideas and techniques. Brewster McCloud (Bud Cort), as conceived by Altman, is a veritable combination of Nietzschean superman and "Our Gang" simp. In addition to the character's boyish charm, there also appears to be a good deal of Altman's own personal world view in this unusual protagonist, whose goal it is to fly above the conventions of society (although many of these parallels are obscured by the film's allegorical overtones). While many of these overtones relate to myths (i. e. , the Icarus and Daedalus myth, "the fall, " etc. ), on the whole, Brewster McCloud is especially well suited to be studied in the context of dreams.

From a Jungian point of view, these dreamlike affinities can be best summed up by the notion that certain visionary artists serve their culture in their capacity as societal dreamers. That is, certain types of art have a social function that is twofold--like dreams. According to Jung, these two functions can be summarized in terms of warning signals, and as compensation for whatever is most lacking in a society. Thus, on an admittedly general level, many of Altman's films can be seen to be ultimately based

From Brewster McCloud

on societal dreams (the "collective unconscious" to Jung),
and are thereby oriented toward fulfilling these functions.
More specifically, Brewster McCloud blurs distinctions be
tween illusion and reality in a manner that strives to compensate for what Altman apparently believes is our culture's
failure to stem the tide of entropic conformity.

One way in which Brewster McCloud seeks to accom-
plish this goal is by integrating a highly realistic environment (Houston, and particularly the Astrodome) with the inner experience manifested by Brewster's fantasy of flying.
As a result, Altman's meticulous use of recognizable props
and locations provides Brewster McCloud with a cutting edge
capable of bringing this flight of fantasy back down to earth.
Along with this, Altman uses filmic allusions and other

Brechtian devices to deconstruct the film's illusionist basis,
adding a further measure of complexity to his spectacle.  In
addition to a plethora of filmic references, the most important of these devices include Altman's use of the Bird Lecturer (Rene Auberjonois) and the film's self-reflexive ending.
Improvisation is another modernistic technique that Altman
and his performers play with, a technique, moreover, that
is bolstered by the director's use of a host of actors and
actresses who have come to be closely associated with Altman and his working methods.  Besides Shelley Duvall (in
her first role) and Bert Remsen (McCabe, Thieves, California Split, Nashville, Buffalo Bill, and A Wedding), Brewster
McCloud's cast includes the following performers from
M*A*S*H:  Rene Auberjonois, Bud Cort, Sally Kellerman,
John Schuck, Michael Murphy, Corey Fischer, and G.
Wood--many of whom have appeared in numerous other Altman films.

     Largely due to its youthful ambitiousness, Brewster
McCloud is a film in which both cinematic genius and vapid-
ity freely mingle.  On the one hand, the film advanced Altman's innovative tradition of using sound, both overlapping
and contrapuntal in exciting new ways, a feat that is also
matched by the film's highly imaginative visual style.  On
the other hand, Brewster McCloud mixes a cornucopia of
contemporary social commentary (i. e. , its many references
to Nixon, Agnew, race relations, capitalism, etc. ) with Altman's by-now-familiar examination of the plight of the (inner-
directed) "dreamer" who is defeated by the constricting forces
of an (other-directed) materialist society.  The problem here
is that Altman's "realists" are all outrageous stereotypes,
while the "dreamer" in this case is doomed from the very
start.  This tendency toward polarization indicates a kind of
intellectual indecision, which mars most of the director's
dream-oriented films up until Three Women (1977).  It also
nullifies most of Altman's attempts to generate narrative tension in Brewster McCloud and diminishes the impact of many
of his individual satiric bits.

     And yet, because Brewster McCloud's appeal to our
transcendental urges (for personal freedom) is so energetical-
ly executed, its cumulative effect results in a surprisingly
moving indictment of contemporary society.  Once again, R.
D. Laing provides us with a revealing point of reference, inasmuch as the mad dreamer (Brewster) is transformed into
a (counter) cultural hero.  At the same time, however, this
line of thought brings us back to the problem of the Freudian

norm, the state that the patient/analysand is to be brought
to, which neither Altman nor Laing really deal with.   Hence,
the film's overriding sense of moral ambiguity regarding the
responsibility that one must take for one's actions creates a
sort of void in the work, much as the narrative ambiguity as
to who exactly does the killings (Louise, Brewster, or the
raven) reflects a disinclination to pursue ethical matters beyond a certain point.

        Brewster McCloud does manage to hang together,
though, if looked upon as a dreamlike statement of alienation
and rebellion that attempts to sum up a good measure of the
antiestablishment sentiment of the 1960s.   This applies both
to the film's thematic concerns and to their implementation
on the self-reflexive level of aesthetics.   An apparent jum-
ble of ideas and techniques, upon closer examination the film
reveals itself to have been very precisely constructed.   Besides the use of an archetypal dreamer (Brewster) within
Altman's basic auteurist structure, Brewster McCloud also
manifests the filmmaker's recurrent concern with sex and
death.   Throughout his entire career, Altman has never even
come close to portraying a trouble-free male-female relationship.   Therefore, it is ironic that Brewster McCloud, which
links sex and death so clearly, also contains a male-female
relationship that is idealized to a greater degree than in any
of his other films.   In fact, it is the destruction of this
Oedipal relationship between Brewster and Louise (Sally Kellerman) that leads to the hero's demise.

        Along with Brewster, Louise is one of Altman's most
enigmatic characters.   Developing her role from its stick-
figure outline in Doran William Cannon's original screenplay,
Altman and Brian McKay, Altman's cowriter on McCabe,
have created an almost mythical figure who also, like Brewster, attempts to function "above" the laws of society.   As
Brewster's "protector" or guardian angel, Louise is at least
partially responsible for the series of murders that accrue
during the course of the film, a fact that is substantiated by
her command of the raven whose appearance invariably precedes each crime.   Louise's otherworldly aura also stems
from her role as Brewster's mentor and is emblemized by
the scars on her back, where wings were once presumably
attached.   Brewster, on the other hand, is a more earth-
bound figure, whose hubris (cf. Icarus) cannot mask his
human frailties.

        Brewster McCloud also contains many elements that

border on the "smart-ass and cutie-pie, " although their integration into the text is generally successful.   First and foremost among these is Altman's intermittent use of The Lecturer, who sets the tone of the film from the very beginning.
The film opens with Auberjonois's direct address, which
posits "the subject at hand" in terms of "earth's imprison-
ment" and "man's desire to fly. "  The eccentric Lecturer's
(and I think we can safely assume Altman's) stated desire is
to "isolate the dream. "  This, in turn, is elaborated in
terms of the film's central enigma:  "Was the dream to attain the ability to fly, or was the dream the freedom that
true flight seemed to offer man?"  Throughout the film, The
Lecturer is used to comment on various characters and
events, becoming more and more bird-like as the narrative
progresses.   Invariably, his seriocomic observations relate
characters to birds, and humanity's basic situation to a state
of entrapment brought about by his inability to fly.

A somewhat less effective device is the use of the
ubiquitous bird droppings that are found on the bodies of the
murder victims.   And yet, despite its adolescent repetitiveness, Altman's early employment of such excremental humor
scores points for the accuracy with which it hits his unconcealed targets.   One example of this occurs just after the
opening sequence, when a raven, seen with Brewster, shits
on a newspaper headline that reads, "Agnew:  Society Should
Discard Some U. S. People. "  Similarly, both birds and social commentary figure in most of the killings.   Daphne
Heap (Margaret Hamilton) is a racial bigot whose off-screen
death is initiated when the raven frees her pet birds from
their cage.   Abraham Wright (Stacy Keach) is Brewster's
105-year-old employer, whose demise is related to his mis-
erly methods of bilking residents of a series of rest homes
with names like "The Feathered Nest Sanitarium. "

More importantly, Wright's death is also intimately
related both to Brewster--whom he threatens with a gun in
his last on-screen action--and Louise, at whose feet his lifeless body tumbles after careening through the traffic-ridden
streets of Houston (cf. the traffic pile-up in Nashville) on
his wheelchair.   And because Wright is such an obvious
caricature, it is easy for the audience to condone Brewster
and Louise in their implied actions.   The above also applies
to the murder of Douglas Greene, which also occurs off-
screen, as do all the murders.   As played by Bert Remsen,
Narcotics Agent Greene is a wanton bigot of the first order.
As soon as he spies Brewster with his newly stolen Nikon

(at the zoo), he threatens to imprison him on a trumped-up
marijuana charge unless the youth will turn over the camera.   Despite the comic implications that lead up to Greene's
murder, the spectator can no longer ignore the fact that
Brewster's megalomaniacal concerns (he's at the zoo taking
intricate photos of birds' wings) have distracted him from
both the moral and pragmatic reality of his situation.   In
short, he is no "superman."

Nor, for that matter, is Detective Frank Shaft
(Michael Murphy), whom The Lecturer likens to a strutting
peacock.   Called in from San Francisco to investigate the
murders by Houston politico Haskell Weeks (William Windom), Murphy's Shaft is a send-up of Steve McQueen's Bullitt.   Before Paul Mazursky (An Unmarried Woman) and
Woody Allen (Manhattan) put his idiosyncratic talents to
work, it was Altman's comic sensibility that initially latched
onto Murphy's ability to debunk the myth of the macho male
star.   Improvising much of his dialogue, Murphy's droll
presence is played off against that of John Schuck's idola-
trous traffic cop.   And here, again, although the resultant
humor is somewhat repetitive, Altman does manage to generate several chuckles from the misadventures of this curiously nonessential character.   The best of these comic moments comes during Shaft's introduction, when he unpacks a
seemingly endless array of multicolored turtleneck sweaters,
while a radio voice-over tells us how "cool" the man is.

In one of Brewster McCloud's many subplots, Shaft
is also used to satirize the lengths that power-hungry poli-
ticians like Haskell Weeks will go to in order to enhance
their public image.   But because of Shaft's narcissistic insistence that he is his own man, Weeks's scheme serves
only to initiate a series of squabbles and petty bickering between himself, Shaft, and Captain Crandall (G. Wood)--an
obvious comment on interagency struggles--which The Lecturer duly mocks in terms of bird imagery.   Other, less
successful ("cutie-pie") elements include the repeated use of
the fat Astrodome guard whose "wings are so short that it
has no power to rise itself from the ground" and Altman's
school-boyish dabblings with marijuana, excrement, and sex.
In this last regard, Altman seems to overextend himself
most clearly in the two scenes in which an oversexed young
girl, Hope (Jennifer Salt), experiences orgasmic bliss from
her mere proximity to Brewster in his subterranean Astrodome hideaway.

Much closer to the mark is the relationship between
Brewster and Suzanne (Shelley Duvall), which also signifies
an important shift in Altman's linear sequence.   Like Hope--
who steals health foods to provide Brewster with sustenance--
Suzanne's whimsical sense of immorality (she's not at all
concerned when she catches Brewster trying to steal the car
that she herself has virtually stolen) immediately ingratiates
her with both Brewster and the viewer.   Unlike the viewer,
however, Brewster soon falls under Suzanne's sexual influence, a plight that portends the beginning of the end, for
his sexual desire for Suzanne blinds him to the fact that her
other-directed sense of immorality is symptomatic of everything that he is trying to escape.   Brewster's newly acquired
delusions are hinted at by both the senselessness of the next
murder, which occurs after Brewster is threatened by the
rightful owner of Suzanne's car, and Brewster and Suzanne's
subsequent visit to an amusement park called "Lost World."

It is from "Lost World" that Altman initiates a protracted chase sequence (shades of Bullitt) that brings together
many of his major characters.   In addition to the slapstick
crack-ups and slow-motion stunts that ensue, this sequence
culminates in Shaft's terminal humiliation.   This transpires
after Louise forces him off the road--he crashes spectacu-
larly into a pond within earshot of Crandall, Mrs. Greene,
and several others--and Shaft, one "piercing" blue eye (obviously a contact lens) missing, decides to put an end to it
all.   Following this, Altman includes a key sequence that
cuts back and forth between Brewster and Suzanne, and
Brewster and Louise.   While Brewster confides in Suzanne
about his plans to fly away, the shot cuts, although their
dialogue continues over this, to Brewster working on his
wings in his room at the Dome.   Here, Louise warns him
about Suzanne and asks him not to see her again.   Cutting
back to Brewster and Suzanne, Altman substantiates Louise's
warnings by having Suzanne (in an inverted close-up) go on
and on about the profits that could be extracted from Brewster's invention.   Then, after Brewster confesses to Suzanne
that he's responsible for the murders, Louise tells him that
"she'll be the death of you."   Finally, Brewster's pronounce-
ment to Suzanne, "I love you ... and Louise was wrong,"
elicits a bird-like cry from Louise, who walks off with the
raven.

Brewster's rejection of his guardian angel seals his
fate.   Suzanne informs on him and the cops converge on the
Astrodome just as Brewster is about to make his fateful

flight.   Looking up at the domed ceiling, it is obvious that
there is no way out.   His wings hit a guide wire and he
plummets straight down, confirming the Lecturer's hysterical
assertion that humanity will never attain mastery of the air.
Brewster's "fall" leads into a self-reflexive, Fellini-like fi-
nale, which, because of Brewster McCloud's allegorical overtones, is far more successful than the ending of M*A*S*H.
After a moment of silence, a crowd of people begin to cheer,
and the camera pulls back to reveal a circus troop on the
floor of the Dome.   William Windom is the ringmaster who
"proudly presents" the cast of Brewster McCloud, dressed
as circus characters, ending with "Mr. Bud Cort."   At this
point the camera pans down to Cort, who is playing dead,
still dressed as Brewster, and the film ends.


## Images (1972)


Abandoning the allegorical approach to dreams that
characterized Brewster McCloud, Images is a more natural
extension of the kind of subjective fantasies first explored
in That Cold Day in the Park.   Moreover, Images takes the
fantasy/reality dichotomy one step farther than That Cold
Day by blurring distinctions between these two poles in a
manner that makes it impossible to know whether the events
we are witnessing are "real" or whether they are a product
of the heroine's imagination (Cathryn, played by Susannah
York).   Once again, sex and death are prominent thematic
elements, although this time around it is Cathryn's inability
to have children that serves as the main cause of her psychological imbalance.   By the same token, however, Images
(like That Cold Day) also makes it clear that it is not a
clinical case study, but rather a dreamlike rendering of a
particular kind of individual madness.

Altman has said that Images resembles a geometric
figure. 6  If so, it is my contention that the film can be
looked upon as a ("vicious") circle, and that its central preoccupation with structural ambiguity fails to mask its many
conceptual deficiencies.   For although style can, and in Altman's films quite often does, convey its own distinct patterns
of meaning, Images's stylistic treatment of ambiguity results
in a fetishistic display of obscurity for obscurity's sake.   To
be sure, the film also contains many redeeming qualities,
but by and large its major problems can be seen to reside

From Images


in the filmmaker's self-conscious attempts to negate all coherent readings.  At the same time, Images's overdetermined
narrative structures seem to promise some kind of psychological profundity, which That Cold Day's gothic touches did not
really aspire to.  In the final accounting, however, these potential psychological insights are obfuscated by a series of
carefully plotted confusions that leave the spectator, and the
protagonist, in virtually the same place that they started out
in.

        On the narrative level, this notion of Images's circu-
larity is borne out by an apparently minor detail.  Near the
beginning of the film, an unidentified woman on the telephone
tells Cathryn that her husband, Hugh (Rene Auberjonois), is
in bed with another woman.  She gives Cathryn the phone
number and address of the alleged rendezvous, but when
Cathryn calls, the line is busy.  It is not until the film is
nearly over, however, that Altman subtly reveals that both
Cathryn's and the mystery woman's address are one and the
same.  Consequently, the entire film can be reread as a
representation of Cathryn's schizophrenic imagination.

        "Schizophrenic" also provides us with an apt descrip-
tion of Images's impact on the spectator, inasmuch as its
engaging aspects seem to be in constant conflict with its
half-baked pretentions.  First written by Altman in 1967,

Images was a film that the director wanted to do even before
That Cold Day in the Park.   Shot in Ireland, it is also Altman's only film that does not reflect upon the American experience in any way.   In this same vein, the dreamlike
qualities of its primary location provide a striking contrast
to the harsh social realities implied by the settings of Altman's other dream films.   Thus, Images is at once the
filmmaker's most individually oriented work, as well as his
most universal, for even if most of his open spaces lead to
dead ends, the cumulative power of Altman's images, if not
Cathryn's, implies a way out.

      In other words, Altman's demonstration of his own
inner-directed artistry indicates a goal that Cathryn's inability to separate creativity and procreativity prevents her from
achieving.   In this sense, Images goes beyond the Laingian
pessimism of That Cold Day to a conception of "adjustment"
that emphasizes self-actualization and the creative process.
From this point of view, society is not indicted (as it is in
most of Altman's other films that deal with madness) nearly
as strongly as the individual's own lack of awareness.   Accordingly, madness is divested of many of its social ramifications, in the broadest sense, so that Altman may play with
his characters' images much as Cathryn and Susannah play
with their jigsaw puzzle.

      The social level that Images does explore deals pri-
marily with Cathryn's relationships as a cause of her psychosis.   However, such causation is a highly debatable force
in Altman's more dreamlike renderings; one must exercise
extreme caution when applying certain kinds of psychological
methodologies to these films.   The danger is that films such
as Images--whose prime raison d'être is to remain open to
a multiplicity of interpretations--can so easily be reduced to
this or that psychological theory at the expense of its more
expansive qualities and aspirations.   Nevertheless, if we
keep these warnings in mind, it is instructive to observe
that most of Cathryn's problems stem from sexual fear and
guilt and her yearnings for the security of a more traditional family unit.

      Images begins by placing the viewer in the position
of a voyeur, looking in on Cathryn through her window.   As
Cathryn (in voice-over) recites from "In Search of Unicorns,"
a children's book that she is writing, the film's dreamlike
tone is further established by both the camera's highly se-
lective explorations, and John Williams's bizarre musical

score.  In conjunction with the pervasive tinkling of wind
chimes, Altman's overt use of the zoom and his attraction
to a variety of glassy surfaces add to this feeling of narrative uncertainty.  The opening of the film also reveals a
basic structural pattern that will be repeated many times as
the film goes on.  This pattern involves the constant alternation between shots and sequences in which Cathryn appears to
be perfectly rational and those in which her imagination takes
over.  Thus, even after Cathryn's schizophrenia is revealed
very early on, the viewer must still work to distinguish one
level of ("real") events from another ("imaginary").

     The revelation of Cathryn's illness occurs after we
have already been put on our guard by Altman's moody opening and the business of Cathryn's strange female informant.
Hugh returns home, and then suddenly, Cathryn is frightened
by what we must presume to be an apparition of Rene (Marcel Bozzuffi).  Curiously, she calls the apparition a "dream,"
although she was not sleeping, but is unsettled enough to ask
Hugh to take her back "home" to Greencove.  It is here, in
the idyllic setting of Greencove, that Cathryn will undergo
the majority of her mental changes, which bear many affinities with Jung's conception of retreat from societal structures towards psychic renewal.

     This opening section also contains several intimations
of Hugh's ineffectuality, which will reoccur once the couple
have arrived in Greencove.  After Cathryn is startled, in
Greencove, by the sound of something that she later concludes she must be "imagining," Hugh repeats his previous
action of coming up with a particularly bad joke in a time
of crisis.  Displaying just the right blend of perfunctory concern and lack of compassion, Hugh even goes so far as to
(playfully?) frighten Cathryn with a deer's head after searching for the source of the imaginary sound.  Significantly,
this action has been preceded by Cathryn's apparent sighting
of herself, and vice versa, as she enters the abode of her
childhood.  However, this use of doubling is marred (as is
a great deal of Images) by Altman's heavyhanded insistence
on forcing his musical cues on the spectator (cf. That Cold
Day in the Park).  That is, the wind chimes that intermittently accompany most of Cathryn's images become an annoyingly overstated distraction quite early in the film.

     Hugh is an amateur photographer whose superficial
world view is repeatedly associated with the one-dimensional
reality of the photographic image.  One of Altman's more

resonant icons, the still camera, is also used as both a self-referential device (cf. Antonioni's <u>Blow-up</u>) and as a surrogate object upon which Cathryn can vent her frustrations. For example, after Rene reappears at Greencove, Altman zooms in on Hugh's camera as if to question the reality of Cathryn's (and Altman's own) images. Later, after Cathryn has apparently "killed" Rene, her anger is appropriately transferred to this same reproductive device when it turns out that, in eradicating her images of Rene, Cathryn has "actually" managed to demolish her husband's camera.

Meanwhile, Rene has previously been revealed as a semiconscious projection of Cathryn's hyperactive imagination. This transpires when Cathryn addresses her recurrent apparition, saying, "This is not happening. I won't let it happen; you've been dead for three years...." It is at this point that Rene, or Cathryn's subconscious, lays out her fundamental problem quite succinctly, telling Cathryn that although she can't become pregnant, there's nothing wrong with her "physically." Moreover, her rejoinder that she only wanted a baby and didn't really cheat on Hugh makes it relatively clear that frustration and guilt are at the root of her illness.

Although these observations point toward a sexually based, Freudian-type theory as providing an explanation for schizophrenia, it is important to note the extent to which the protagonist's problems may be the result of her more subtly stated creative frustrations. For instance, <u>Images</u> begins and ends with excerpts from the book that Cathryn is writing. And while the fact that "In Search of Unicorns" (which was written by Susannah York) is ostensibly for children implies that Cathryn is attempting to compensate for her inability to have any, her repetitious recitations also imply an inability to achieve this other, more creative goal. In other words, because "In Search of Unicorns," for which Jung would seem the most appropriate psychological referent, is such a tediously revealing affair, it is difficult not to interpret it as a major source of Cathryn's frustrations. Additionally, Cathryn never actually finishes her book (the girl Susannah does), just as it is Susannah (played by Cathryn Harrison) who completes the jigsaw puzzle that was Cathryn's as a child and has Cathryn stymied.

Susannah is a "real" apparition whose remarkable physical resemblance to Cathryn suggests a projection of the

protagonist's regressive self. This is first intimated by the
way that Cathryn discovers the young girl hiding in a closet--
a striking image of self-recognition that Cathryn initially re-
coils from. As it turns out, Susannah is the daughter of
Marcel (Hugh Millais), another ex-lover, whom Cathryn proceeds to confuse with Rene. Shortly thereafter, Altman
combines many of his previously established motifs in a
scene in which Cathryn works on the jigsaw puzzle (accompanied by her voice-over recitation) at the same time that
Marcel relates the story of his wife's unfaithfulness. The
scene then concludes with a series of shots of the still camera, the puzzle, Cathryn, and Susannah, as Cathryn finally
comes out of her reveries. On a subjective level, the effect of this combination of elements seems to unsettle Cathryn somewhat, but she is nevertheless lucid enough to ward
off Marcel's subsequent advances with the assertion that, although she knows she's been "sick," she still loves her husband. When Cathryn asks Hugh to make love to her, however, her efforts to reaffirm that relationship are dashed by
her husband's inebriated lack of concern.

These actions set the stage for a sequence in which
Cathryn's confused sense of sexual identity reaches its peak.
After her rejection by Hugh, Cathryn embraces Rene, who
changes to Marcel, and then to Hugh. Murmuring that she
"just wants a baby," Cathryn proceeds to engage in sexual
relations, but the identity of her partner is obscured by Altman's shifts in focus. When these blurry images clear,
Cathryn is looking at herself in the mirror. Entering her
bedroom, she apparently confuses Hugh with an image of her
voluptuous, "shadow" self, and screams, unable to accept
this repressed vision of herself. The next day, this afore-
mentioned confusion is compounded by Marcel, who asks
her, "What or who got into you last night?" Then Rene reappears, smirking about how "fantastic" she was the previous evening. It is at this point that Cathryn obliterates Rene
with Hugh's rifle, but when Susannah and a stranger rush in,
Hugh's mangled camera is the only tangible sign that something is amiss.

Returning to his strategy of alternation, Altman follows Cathryn's subsequent ruminations about her "soul" (from
"In Search of Unicorns") with Susannah's complaint that she
won't be able to finish the puzzle because too many pieces
are missing. Although Cathryn locates the missing pieces,
the success of her mini-search is immediately undercut by
Marcel's sudden appearance. Confused by his references to

their activities on the previous night, Cathryn goes from
cool to hot to cool in very short order, which prompts Marcel to label her a "schizo." As if to confirm his, or her
own, observation, Cathryn goes downstairs and gets a knife
(cf. That Cold Day), but when she returns to the room, only
Hugh is there. Realizing that Marcel's visitation may have
been a figment of her imagination, Cathryn now attempts to
puzzle out her irrationality in a paradoxically logical manner.
However, although Susannah confirms Cathryn's suspicions
that Marcel had been downstairs the whole time, Cathryn's
efforts to achieve a sense of clarity and wholeness are strikingly subverted by a cut to her gazing at her dual images in
a mirror.

Returning to the waterfall, which she is becoming increasingly attached to, Cathryn finally confronts her other
self, or vice versa, but little is resolved by her screams
for her double to "go back!" It is interesting to note, however, that as soon as Cathryn returns to the house, it is
Hugh who announces that he has to "go back" to work (to
town) for a few days. Cathryn declines his offer to come
along (she says she has to finish her book), and then actually encourages him to leave her, while the camera sugges-
tively moves past a rack of kitchen knives. After dropping
Hugh at the station, Cathryn goes for one of the knives, just
before Marcel appears, asking how she got rid of Hugh.
Now, both the order and the nature of these actions imply
that Cathryn is attempting to exorcize Marcel, and possibly
Hugh, from her psyche, as she replies that "I thought him
away just like I thought you here." Next, Cathryn stabs
Marcel, and walks upstairs, smiling at her new-found sense
of control.

The next morning, Altman complicates matters even
further by including a suspense ploy in which a neighbor and
his dog show up at Cathryn's front door (while Marcel's lifeless body is still visible on the floor). Moments later, Altman even goes so far as to have Cathryn shoo the dog away
from the scent of the (imaginary?) corpse, an action that
undermines Cathryn's most recent epiphany. Consequently,
when Susannah reappears, looking for her father, Cathryn
virtually forces the young girl to assuage her fears by having Susannah assert that she saw Marcel late that last night.
When Susannah complies, Cathryn's relief manifests itself
in the disappearance of Marcel's corpse.

The film's concluding sequences are equally cryptic.

After seeing Marcel in the flesh, Cathryn now feels that she
"knows" she has been a victim of her own schizophrenic imagination. Thus, it is a newly confident Cathryn who runs
her double off the road, over the cliff near the waterfall.
The fact that her problems are far from over, however, is
subtly indicated by Cathryn's subsequent phone conversation,
in which it "appears" that she has been talking to herself.
Following Cathryn's disjointed ride back to town, these mis-
givings are confirmed by the sudden reappearance of Cathryn's other self, accompanied by the neighbor's dog. Her
double denies Cathryn's claim to having killed her, at which
point Cathryn screams, and the shot dissolves to the waterfall and Hugh's body at the bottom. Finally, Susannah's
voice-over finishes the book at the very same moment that
she places the last piece in the puzzle (end credits).

In the end, though, the cumulative weight of Images's
ambiguous narrative structures make it impossible to explain
the entire film in terms of what may seem to be its most
convincing murder. In view of all that has preceded it,
there is simply no way of ascertaining whether Hugh is, in
fact, the real victim of Cathryn's guilt-ridden psychosis.
Similarly, most doctrinaire attempts to "explain away" Cathryn's psychological problems will inevitably close more doors
than they open. What we are left with, then, resembles an
intricately constructed puzzle in which style serves as both
a means and an end. By the same token, the major trouble
with this construction (this "circle") is that for all her erot-
ic appeal, Cathryn is even less engaging than Sandy Dennis's
loquacious spinster in That Cold Day in the Park. More
specifically, Cathryn's humorless babblings about the "soul"
are so painfully trivial and boring, that we soon cease to
care about her problems. Then, too, Altman's stylistic attempts, especially his use of music, to engage us in her
psychic flounderings are often cumbersome and labored.

One prime example of what might be considered Altman's "smart-ass" pretensions is contained in the way that
all the major characters and actors swap names. For instance, Cathryn is played by Susannah York while Susannah
is played by Cathryn Harrison. Also, Rene Auberjonois plays
Hugh, Hugh Millais plays Marcel, and Marcel Bozzuffi plays
Rene. And yet, for all its pretentions, Altman's (and Zsigmond's et al.) highly personal style still offers the viewer a
number of exquisite images, as well as a fair share of compelling dramatic moments. Thus, Images's self-assertive
strategy ultimately results in a kind of aesthetic stalemate

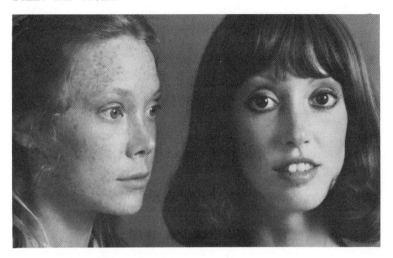

From Three Women

at best, which seems to have enabled Altman to exorcize
many of his own demons.   Accordingly, it was not until five
years later that Altman returned to the dream mode, in
Three Women, by which time he was able to avoid many of
the reductive devices that obscured the imaginative potential
of Images.

### Three Women (1977)

The most striking difference between Images and
Three Women is undoubtedly the more recent film's greater
sense of fluidity.   To be sure, they both have many similarities (Zsigmond's and Chuck Rosher's brilliant images, ex-
cessive use of "strange" music, and their many affinities
with dreams), but on the whole it is Three Women's ability
to integrate more freely its formal level without always
straining for effect that makes it a superior film. 7   More
specifically, Three Women's success is largely the result
of two central factors that were missing from Images.   The
first involves Shelley Duvall's extraordinary portrayal of
Millie Lammoreaux, a rather ordinary young woman whom
Duvall manages to transform into a character of great
warmth and dignity.   The second has to do with Altman's

use of his Palm Desert, California, location, which provides
this dreamlike drama with a highly realistic cutting edge.
Once again, Three Women's setting brings the filmmaker
back to an examination of the kind of fundamental American
experience (cf. Nashville, A Wedding, Brewster McCloud,
McCabe, Thieves, etc.) upon which his talents seem to
thrive.   Together, these two factors help to supply Three
Women with the type of solid foundation necessary to support
Altman's more abstract concerns with transference and rebirth.   Moreover, because Three Women charts the moral
and emotional growth of its protagonists, rather than their
deterioration, it more closely approximates the synergistic
goal of constructive interaction than Images.

Just as Images starts off with Cathryn's recitation,
Three Women begins with a series of shots of paintings by
Willie (Janice Rule).   Similarly, along with Gerald Busby's
"mood" music, it is the unusual content of these murals
(done by Bodhi Wind) that sets the tone of the film.   That
is, although it is too soon to "interpret" them, the primitive
anthropomorphism of Willie's figures are definitely "the stuff
that dreams are made of."   Consequently, when Altman cuts
to a series of live-action shots, without including diegetic
sounds, of Millie (Duvall) being observed by Pinky (Sissy
Spacek) at the health spa, these images also take on a dreamlike quality by association.   Additionally, it is worth noting
at this point that Altman has repeatedly stated that he literally envisioned Three Women in a dream.

From the outset, it is Pinky who appears to be the
film's controlling dreamer.   This is implied in a variety of
ways, the most notable of which are the atonal musical cues
that accompany many of her early actions.   As we soon find
out, Pinky is an extremely impressionable and underdeveloped
personality type, while Millie is all personality.   Accordingly, it seems quite natural when Pinky's instant admiration for
Millie expresses itself in several acts of obvious mimicry.
In broad terms, one might even say that from the very start,
Pinky "dreams" of becoming Millie.   As Altman articulates
it, however, the "catch-22" of Pinky's aspirations resides in
her failure to realize that Millie's personality is an almost
totally artificial creation of the media.   In other words,
there is no real Millie to model herself after other than the
archetypal consumer who lists her recipes by how long they
take to make and whose greatest joy in life is the arrival of
the latest catalogue from Neiman-Marcus.

Although these two women appear to be cut from radically different molds (according to Altman, Pinky and Millie are the "three women" of the title), Altman also includes a number of early hints that point toward their sameness. Becoming more overt as the film progresses, the first of these indications comes in the form of the same line that Julie Christie addressed to Shelley Duvall in McCabe and Mrs. Miller: "You're little, like me." In the present instance, however, Duvall's/Millie's comment to Pinky, while fitting her with a swimsuit at the spa, is considerably more resonant. The second clue is dropped by Dr. Maas (Craig Richard Nelson) who observes that the two young women should get along since they're both from Texas. But the real clincher doesn't come until Pinky tells Edgar (Robert Fortier) that her real name is Mildred and that she hates it, this to Millie's disgust.

This last action occurs at "Dodge City," the ramshackle remnants of a desert tourist trap owned by Edgar and Willie. It is here that one of Altman's strange musical cues first draws our attention to Willie, whose eye contact with Pinky is underscored by a zoom-in from the younger woman's point of view. Then, after Millie tricks Pinky with a horrendously ugly mechanical toy, "Dirty Gertie," Millie's soulessness is hinted at in her description of Willie and Edgar. That is, she tells Pinky not to pay any attention to Willie, who "doesn't talk much," but adds that Edgar's lots of fun: "He knows Hugh O'Brian." In contrast, Pinky immediately lets Willie know that she likes her paintings, which everyone else in the film seems oblivious to. Moments later, Pinky finds out just how much fun Edgar can be when the aging "stunt double" fools her with a rubber snake.

When the new roommates arrive at Millie's apartment complex, "The Purple Sage," for the first time together, Pinky spaces out on the weird murals (accompanied by Busby's music) that adorn the bottom of the pool. Millie informs her that Willie painted them a long time ago, and that Willie and Edgar own The Purple Sage. After Millie is blatantly avoided by a neighbor, Tom, whom she claims would like to be her boyfriend, Pinky waxes ecstatic over Millie's "decorated" apartment. Done up in a bright version of the yellow tones that dominate her wardrobe and car, Millie's apartment conveys the same initial impression of cheerful well-being as her carefully programmed persona.

Pinky, on the other hand, is first characterized by light
pink, and later by a more mature rose.  This transformation is significant inasmuch as Willie is also associated with
primary colors, especially red.  Finally, The Purple Sage
itself supplies a disconcerting variation on these pinkish-red
hues, which fits in well with the unusual events that are
about to transpire there.

        At the apartment, Pinky's feelings about Millie are
reaffirmed when she calls her "the most perfect person that
I ever met."  Similarly, Pinky's burgeoning attraction to
Willie is also underscored, albeit in a much more cryptic
manner.  This occurs when Altman inserts a shot, accompanied by Busby's music, of Pinky observing Willie through
the water and glass of Millie's aquarium.  Then, following
Millie's mild, but apparently accurate, put-down of Pinky
(recited in voice-over by Millie) in her diary, Altman zooms
in to a shadowy close-up of Pinky before cutting to the murals and a facsimile of the previous shot of Willie through
the aquarium.  In effect, these last dreamlike images, of
the murals, water, and Willie, begin to point toward Willie
as what the Jungians refer to as Pinky's "shadow" (the con-
tainer of one's repressions or negative energy).  Moreover,
because Willie is to closely related to pools and water, the
life blood of the desert, Altman is able suitably to symbolize
the potential for psychological regeneration (Willie is also
pregnant) in terms of the acceptance of one's shadow.

        Thus far, however, Pinky is hardly aware of the
strange power that Willie and her creations are beginning to
exert upon her.  So it is that when Millie goes out for a
date, Pinky goes straight for the other woman's diary.
Meanwhile, Millie returns home early, having evidently been
stood up.  But even though Millie vents her frustrations
(she's also been taking it on the chin from her neighbors)
on her roommate, Pinky remains totally wrapped up in her
Millie fantasies.  The next day, the strength of this growing
obsession manifests itself when Pinky "mistakenly" punches
Millie's card on the way out of work.  Then, on the way to
Dodge City, Pinky's comments about the twins, who also
work at the spa, give further evidence of her unconscious
concern with transference.  Wondering what it's like to be
twins, Pinky suggests that they may be able to switch back
and forth, or "maybe they're just the same one all the
time."

        At Dodge City, Pinky lingers around the empty pool

in which Willie is painting, while Millie joins Edgar at the
shooting range.   Shy and standoffish, Pinky indicates that
she doesn't like guns, while lecherous Edgar instructs Millie on the art of target shooting.   This scene is most noteworthy for Edgar's retrospectively ironic comment that he'd
"rather face a hundred savages than one woman who's
learned how to shoot."   Back at the shack, Millie tells Pinky
that Deirdre, her ex-roommate, and her boyfriend are coming over for one of her "famous" dinner parties.   Reempha-
sizing Millie's consumerism, Altman makes sure that we
notice that everything Millie has bought comes in a can, even
to the point of zooming in on some artificial dessert topping.
While they set the table, Pinky spills some red shrimp cock-
tail on her dress, which causes Millie to go out for another,
because "the table won't be even," even though Pinky says
she won't eat one.   In the interim, Deirdre and her friends
stop by (Deirdre calls Pinky "Red") to say they won't be
able to make it for dinner.   Deflated again, Millie blames
Pinky--"You ruined everything ... you always do"--and takes
off alone for Dodge City.

Following a brief, unexplained sequence, which includes shots of Willie and the murals in the pool, Millie returns home with Edgar.   Shocked by this turn of events,
Pinky is shaken up even further when Millie rails at her,
"What do you know about anything?...   You don't drink, you
don't smoke, you don't do anything right."   This sends Pinky
out on the balcony, crying.   Next, what we must assume to
be Pinky's attempted suicide is preceded by a tilt-down to
the pool (Pinky is reflected in the shimmering water over
the murals), a shot of Pinky raising her arms, and a close-
up of one of the murals.   Accordingly, when Pinky plunges
in, in slow motion, Willie's paintings seem to have almost
as much to do with her actions as did her previous confrontation with Millie and Edgar.

In view of the above, it is not surprising that Willie
is the first person to come to Pinky's aid.   Apparently aware
of her culpability, both Willie's actions and her calls for
help (the first words she has uttered) are indicative of a
kind of rebirth.   Of course, for all pragmatic purposes,
Millie and Edgar are chiefly responsible for Pinky's plunge,
but, typical of Altman's treatment of men in Three Women,
Edgar is incapable of displaying any kind of real emotion.
Millie, on the other hand, is extremely distraught and will
soon undergo an even more radical transformation than the
one that Willie is going through.   Thus, after Millie passes

Willie, whose image has been doubly reflected in a glass
screen, in the hospital, her own "rebirth" is anticipated by
a similar shot of Millie's split reflection, while she cries.
In a brilliant touch, Altman even has Millie refuse a young
intern's offer of breakfast, something the old Millie would
never have done under any circumstances.   But the real
beauty of this scene is the way in which it reveals, in part
through the doctor's very offer, that this new, more emotional Millie is a much more appealing person.

Concentrating more and more on Millie now, although
by this point in the narrative all three women are inextric-
ably related, Altman proceeds to chronicle Millie's search
for Pinky's parents.   After she finally picks up the old
couple (played by John Cromwell and Ruth Nelson) at the bus
depot, Altman then inserts an ambiguous line of dialogue
that refers back to Pinky's prior observations on the similarity between the California desert landscape and Texas.
Thus, when Mrs. Rose says that "it sure doesn't look like
Texas," the effect is strangely unsettling.   Even more jarring for Millie is the Roses' enactment of the primal scene,
which Millie subsequently witnesses (as the camera zooms
in) in her apartment.   Next, the viewer is almost physiolog-
ically implicated in this prevailing disquietude by means of
a shock cut marked by the piercing sound of gunshots.
These sounds are caused by Willie, looking very pregnant,
who fires several shots at her paintings before switching to
a humanoid target.   Without pausing, Altman proceeds to
cut to the hospital, where Pinky's new self--"Don't call me
Pinky!"--denies that the Roses are her parents.   In the
abovementioned sequence of events, both Altman's editing
patterns, from Millie to Willie to Pinky, and the discordant
actions of all three women serve to link them even more
closely together.

When she returns from the hospital, Pinky's initial
transformation is almost complete.   This is first indicated
by the blood-red color that she now paints her toenails, and
later, by the way that she contrives to take over Millie's
room.   But rather than having become Millie, Pinky's present incarnation is suggestive of the shadow archetype that
haunts each of the three women.   This is implied by the
fact that she, too, begins to make time with Edgar.   Em-
blemizing the negative aspects of this turn of events, Altman
concludes his brief depiction of Pinky and Edgar's drunken
tryst, which Millie is unaware of, with a zoom-in to Pinky
imitating Dirty Gertie's satanic laughter.   Meanwhile, Pinky's

behavior is slowly but surely drawing Millie closer to Willie.
Thus, it isn't long before Pinky's previous attraction to the
murals is transferred to Millie by means of an earlier visual strategy: the use of zooms to signify point of view.

In her more vulnerable state, Millie's victimization
is repeatedly connected with groups of two, which reflect
her current split. In addition to Dr. Maas and his female
colleague at the spa, the two cops who answer Millie's call
when her car is stolen provide a particularly interesting
variation on this motif. That is, both their familiarity--
they both hang out at Dodge City--and incredulity work to
create a conspiratorial mood that threatens to undermine
Millie's tenuous mental balance. Similar in effect to the
surreptitious murmurings of the numerous twosomes at the
spa, especially the twins, the cops' attitudes strategically
preface Millie's discovery that Pinky has "stolen" her car.
Although this discovery appears to legitimize the officers'
skepticism, in Millie's mind, the sight of Pinky, dressed
in "hot pink," being instructed on the target range by Edgar, subconsciously confirms her feeling that some part of
herself is being "ripped off." The pattern is clear: first
her name, "Mildred," then her bed, her car, and now her
ex-lover have all been appropriated. Additionally, Millie
is on the verge of succumbing to the same kind of paranoid
delusions, also associated with the murals, that led to
Pinky's plunge.

At The Purple Sage, Pinky has managed to become
the "popularity queen" that Millie had always wanted to be.
Joining in with the crowd, she again spurns Millie, leaving
her roommate to fend for herself. It is at this point that
Millie's discovery that her diary has also been appropriated
confirms her latent suspicions that Pinky has gone over the
line. More specifically, Pinky's comments, in Millie's
diary, about her parents eliminate any lingering doubts as
to whether or not Pinky is putting on an act. [8] The only
problem is that Millie is at a loss as to how she should
deal with Pinky's schizophrenia. After Pinky chides Millie
for reading "her" diary, however, Millie's course of action
is greatly influenced by Pinky's subsequent nightmare.

Three Women's longest overt dream sequence, this
nightmare, is preceded by a zoom-in to an extreme close-
up of Millie that would seem to indicate that she is actually
doing the dreaming. The images that follow all relate back
to earlier scenes: Willie superimposed over rippling water,

the twins at the spa, Willie's and Millie's doubly reflected
images from the hospital, murals in the pool, Pinky with
her parents, Millie and Pinky at the shooting range, and,
finally, Pinky floating face down in the pool.   But although
the dream began just after the abovementioned close-up of
Millie, it is immediately followed by a scene in which Pinky
tells Millie that she's been frightened by a dream. Consequently, we must assume that it is Pinky's subconscious
recollections that precipitate yet another fluid (more so than
the dream itself) transformation in both women.   That is,
the way in which Pinky responds to Millie's reassurances
that "dreams can't hurt you" appears to indicate that Pinky's
childishly rebellious ego has been tamed by the more mature
mother figure that Millie has come to represent.

   After the dream, these changes are also reflected in
the way that Millie orders Edgar out of her apartment, while
Pinky cowers behind her (mother).   Similarly, when Edgar
tells them that Willie is having her baby, it is Millie who
leads Pinky out by the hand, in an attempt to come to the
deserted woman's aid.   Because it is already too late to get
Willie to the hospital, Millie sends Pinky for a doctor, while
she begins to help with the delivery.   Meanwhile, Pinky never manages to get more than ten yards away from the house,
where she merely stops to observe the subsequent action.
What she sees and hears at this point is particularly poignant, inasmuch as Millie, for all her resoluteness, hasn't
the foggiest notion of what she should do.   At the same
time, Pinky's own actions (or inaction) seem to be motivated
by a curious (because it is not necessarily conscious) desire
to revenge herself on Willie.

   Of course, there are several other possible explanations for Pinky's behavior, but, true to form, the blurry
quality of Altman's (and Chuck Rosher's) depiction of this
sequence underlies the senselessness of trying to come up
with a definitive answer.   Moreover, although Pinky's par-
tial responsibility for the baby's death (he's stillborn) is
clearly articulated, her motives are never really questioned
by any of the other characters.   In metaphysical terms,
however, the baby's death, along with Edgar's, is most
definitely a catalyst for the final rebirth of all three women.

   After Millie slaps Pinky for her failure to fetch a
doctor, Altman eschews the kind of "smart-ass" transitions
that marred Images in favor of a more fluid means of bridg-
ing the action.   Accordingly, the lazy shots of a Coca-Cola

truck approaching Dodge City give the spectator pause to
relax after the intense emotional tumult of the previous
scene.   Because Three Women is so clearly about change,
what is most intriguing about this introduction to the film's
epilogue is the way that it conveys an impression of stasis.
Thus, the intimation that certain things (symbolized by the
desert and Coca-Cola) never seem to change, actually works
to set the viewer up for the revelation of the radical (inter-
personal) transformations that each of the three women has
undergone.

       Languishing behind the counter of the Dodge City bar,
Pinky barely looks up from her magazine as the driver of
the Coca-Cola truck enters.   When he asks her to sign an
order form, she says she'll get her mom, who turns out to
be none other than Millie, dressed very much like Willie.
Then, the delivery man mentions something about not understanding the "accident," Edgar having been so good with guns
and all.   At this point, it becomes fairly obvious that the
women--each of whom he has wronged--have somehow managed to kill Edgar (remember his comment on facing "a
hundred savages").   And despite--or rather because of--the
death of Edgar and the baby, Altman gives us every indication that the women have found a kind of contentment that
none of them had ever known.   That is, although their newly
formed family unit (Willie as Grandma, Millie and Pinky as
mother and daughter) hardly leads an idyllic existence, their
present conflicts are extremely minor.   This is conveyed
via bits of mother-daughter banter that, together with the
women's outfits, connotes a healthy pioneer-like spirit rather
than the feeling of real animosity.

       Willie's mental health is particularly noticeable, inas-
much as she is now able to speak freely and communicate
positive emotions.   This is confirmed when she tells Pinky
that she just had "the most wonderful dream" (Three Wom-
en?), but that she can no longer remember it.   Thus, when
Willie tells Millie not to be so mean to Pinky, it is, like
the byplay between Millie and Pinky, more of an assertion
of family solidarity than a reproof.   That this last line of
dialogue (the last line in the film) is spoken over a pan past
a heap of derelict tires also reaffirms the feeling of new
life amidst the ruins.   Three Women ends with a static shot
of one of Willie's murals.   Slowly fading as the credits begin to roll by, the mural depicts a primordial conflict between three tailed figures of indeterminate sex, one of which
is flanked by a fourth, more masculine, figure, which stands
while the others kneel.

Although Three Women's conclusion is open-ended,
the resultant ambiguity is not distancing or contrived, as it
is in Images.   Once again, the main reasons for this revolve around Altman's overall use of a realistic environment
and the fluidity with which his main characters' personalities
are interchanged.   Along with Altman, a great deal of credit
for the successful visualization of Three Women is also due
cinematographer Chuck Rosher (A Wedding).   In the end,
however, Three Women's major accomplishment lies in Shelley Duvall's portrayal of Millie Lammoreaux.   Improvising
many of her lines, Duvall is consistently brilliant as she
takes Millie on her inward journey from an "other" to an
"inner-directed" survivor, who transcends the barrenness
of her environment once she gets in touch with the latent
power of her subconscious.   Of course, her self-actualization could not have occurred without either Pinky (the
"dreamer"), or Willie, who creates the dreamlike images
that have so much to do with the other two women's transformation.   In fact, by the end of the film, all three characters have come very close to merging into one complete
personality (cf. Pinky's earlier comments about the twins).

On a personal level, the use of women as the main
protagonists in three out of four of his dream films seems
to indicate Altman's association of the feminine archetype
with the subconscious's creative potential.   That is, his
absorption in this archetype is yet another manifestation of
the director's attempt to better understand and integrate his
own personality (psychic whole) through the creative process.
It is these aspirations and the analogous potential that their
actualization in celluloid offers up to the spectator that most
closely link Altman with such European modernists as Buñuel
and Bergman.   Finally, whereas Images bears a strained
resemblance to the best of the European art films, Three
Women evinces a more mature American filmmaker's ability
to create a highly personal work of art.


NOTES


[1]Marsha Kinder, "The Art of Dreaming in Three
Women and Providence:   Structures of the Self," Film Quarterly, Fall 1977, p. 10.
[2]Ibid, p. 12.
[3]Ibid, p. 13.

[4]Michael Dempsey, review of That Cold Day in the Park, in Film Quarterly, Fall 1969, p. 56.

[5]This was hinted at earlier, in a scene in which Frances goes to a health clinic for birth-control pills.

[6]Michel Ciment and Michael Henry, "Entretien avec Robert Altman," Positif 197, p. 14.

[7]One other similarity between Images and Three Women is that they are the only two "post-TV" films for which Altman receives sole screenwriting credit, a fact that is indicative of their highly personal nature.

[8]Pinky writes about her parents as if she were Millie.

# CHAPTER V

## CONCLUSION

As in the fine arts, there are many justifications for viewing the overall pattern of film culture since the 1970s in the context of a "postmodernist" movement. Once many of the techniques popularized by the New Wave became absorbed by the mainstream film and television industries, manifestations of the kinds of open-ended films elaborated upon in this study became fewer and far between. Another explanation for this change was offered by Susan Sontag when she said that contemporary audiences have simply become less willing to be serious "in that old-fashioned way that modernist art demands." And yet, Altman's prolific output (fourteen films) over the past ten years seems to testify to the fact that the modernist tradition in American filmmaking is not completely dead. For even though a good many of his films do not achieve the synergistic ideal of total integration, Altman's daring attempts to provide the viewer with a series of open-ended cinematic experiences have kept an incredibly potent form of filmmaking in the American public eye.

Inasmuch as one of the underlying themes of this study has to do with what I would describe as "the modernist's dilemma," it should be quite clear by now that I feel Altman has come very close to a practical solution. On the one hand, then, I have tended to emphasize his role as a modernist survivor who has consistently refused to capitulate to the demands of the commercial marketplace. But despite my belief that Altman very closely approximates what psychologist Otto Rank has referred to as the "artist-hero," this work has not been aimed at creating yet another culture myth. Instead, I have been most concerned with describing the specific ways in which Altman's films constitute a very real contribution to our culture. First and foremost, this contribution has been seen to involve Altman's repeated attempts to implicate the audience actively in the process of creation.

156

Despite its inexactitude, I have found Arthur Koestler's coinage of the term "bisociation" to be the most useful in elucidating what this process is all about. For although bisociation tends to imply two levels of meaning or interpretation, I have attempted to stress its broader, or more infinite implications vis-à-vis the potential for spectator interaction. In this same vein, the term "open structures" has been employed mainly as a connotative key to what is meant by the synergistic, or cooperative, experience of the artwork. Finally, it has been posited that if such an experience is to occur at all, the work must also display a sense of integration that encompasses each of its structural levels.

At this point, I would like to summarize briefly my personal preferences in regard to the films that have already been discussed. Bearing in mind that Altman's reliance on bisociative themes and structures is largely responsible for the unusually diverse evaluations that his films engender, my own personal pantheon would begin with an upper echelon that includes McCabe and Mrs. Miller, Nashville, and The Long Goodbye. Nashville achieves this distinction largely through the use of highly experimental narrative structures and techniques, while McCabe does so by centering on a more traditionally romantic identification figure. In both cases, however, the net result is a stirringly original cinematic experience that encourages us to examine many of our own preconceptions about filmmaking, our society, and ourselves. Similarly, in bidding farewell to many of the outmoded conventions of the hardboiled detective genre, The Long Goodbye encourages viewers to use the filmic experience as a way of reassessing their feelings about a wide range of filmic and nonfilmic codes.

One notch below these films comes Thieves Like Us and Three Women. Despite its lack of dramatic tension, Thieves is particularly notable for the way it uses authentic period detail to support its wryly lyrical critique of the "American dream." Contravening many of the standard components of the gangster movie, Thieves also stands out as an excellent example of how Altman's revelation of his protagonist's lack of self-awareness offers the spectator a structural invitation to transcend the ordinary state of consciousness. Thieves Like Us also provides us with a marked contrast to such postmodernist tours de force as Coppola's The Godfather I and II, which, whatever way you slice it, spend most of their time glorifying their charismatic heroes.

Taking an entirely different approach to a similar range of problems, Three Women represents Altman's most successful attempt to utilize dream modes as a means of reaffirming the regenerative powers of the self.   Following Thieves and Three Women, Brewster McCloud, the much underrated Quintet, California Split, Buffalo Bill, and That Cold Day in the Park all strike me as relatively successful attempts to extend Altman's formal approach to his art. Admittedly, each of the films included in this third echelon have their own particular failings, but on the whole, each of them also displays a sense of freshness and originality that more than compensates for these drawbacks.   Right behind them, I would list Images, A Wedding, and M*A*S*H, with A Perfect Couple bringing up the rear.

This investigation has, I hope, made it clear that the synergistic potential that I have attributed to Altman's films demands far more than approaching the medium with some "bisociative" meanings in mind, and then sitting back to watch them spread through the collective unconscious.   This point of view is substantiated by the failure of Altman's less successful projects to achieve the level of integration necessary to elicit a truly cooperative response.   Still, it is difficult to overstate the fact that Altman's accomplishments are largely the result of this filmmaker's steadfast refusal to play it safe.   For, unlike most of his contemporaries, Altman has never ceased to attack the formal boundaries of the medium in which he works, regardless of the financial consequences.   At the same time, Altman's ultimate importance rests in his intuitive grasp of his public function as the creator of potentially synergistic (private) experiences that can satisfy the highest criteria of both art and entertainment.

# SELECTED BIBLIOGRAPHY

## 1. Books and Screenplays

Altman, Robert, and Rudolf, Alan. Buffalo Bill and the Indians or Sitting Bull's History Lesson. New York: Bantam, 1976.

Hardin, Nancy, ed. On Making 'a Movie: Brewster McCloud. New York: New American Library, 1971.

Kass, Judith M. Robert Altman: American Innovator. New York: Popular Library, 1978.

## 2. Articles, Interviews, and Reviews

Auwerter, Russell. An untitled interview with Robert Altman, Directors in Action, Bob Thomas, ed. New York: Bobbs-Merrill, 1973.

Benayoun, Robert. Review of Images. Positif 140, July-August 1972.

_____. Reviews of The Long Goodbye and Thieves Like Us. Positif 155, January 1974.

_____. "Altman, U. S. A. " Positif 176, December 1975.

Bourget, Jean-Louis. "Pinky sauvee des hommes (sur 3 Femmes)," Positif 197, September 1977.

Brackett, Leigh. "From 'The Big Sleep' and 'The Long Goodbye' and More or Less How We Got There. " Take One 4, January 1974.

Burgess, Jackson. Review of McCabe and Mrs. Miller. Film Quarterly, Winter 1971-72.

159

_____ . Review of Brewster McCloud. Film Quarterly,
Winter 1971-72.

Ciment, Michel. Review of M*A*S*H from "Cannes 1970."
Positif 118, Summer 1970.

_____ . "Entretien avec Robert Altman." Positif 147,
February 1973.

_____ . "Jouer avec Altman (rencontres avec Ronee
Blakeley et Keith Carradine). Positif 176, December
1975.

_____ . "Entretien avec Robert Altman." Positif 197,
September 1977.

Combs, Richard. Review of Images. Sight and Sound,
Winter 1972-73.

_____ . "Playing the Game, or Robert Altman and the
Indians." Sight and Sound, Summer 1979.

Corliss, Richard. "Outlaws, Auteurs, and Actors." Interview with Keith Carradine and Shelley Duvall. Film
Comment, May-June, 1974.

Cumbow, Robert C. "Out of the Past." Movietone News
#51, August 1976.

Dauman, Anatole, and Sarre, Jean-Paul. "Pinky Rose,
c'est moi." Positif 197, September 1977.

Dawson, Jan. Review of M*A*S*H. Sight and Sound, Summer 1970.

_____ . Review of McCabe and Mrs. Miller. Sight and
Sound, Autumn 1971.

Dempsey, Michael. Review of That Cold Day in the Park.
Film Quarterly 1, Fall 1969.

_____ . "The Empty Staircase and the Chinese Princess."
Film Comment 10, September-October 1974.

Elsaesser, Thomas. "Ou finit le spectacle? (à propos de
Nashville)." Positif 197, September 1977.

Engle, Gary. "McCabe and Mrs. Miller: Robert Altman's Anti-western." Journal of Popular Film 1, Fall 1972.

Falonga, Mark. Review of Images. Film Quarterly, Summer 1973.

Farber, Stephen. "L. A. Journal." Film Comment 9, September-October 1973.

_____. Review of A Perfect Couple. New West, April 23, 1979.

French, Philip. Review of The Long Goodbye. Sight and Sound, Winter 1973-74.

Goodwin, Michael. Review of McCabe and Mrs. Miller. Take One 2, October 1971.

Greenspun, Roger. Review of Three Women. Film Comment, July-August 1977.

Gregory, Charles. "Altman's The Long Goodbye." Sight and Sound, Spring 1973.

_____. "Knight Without Meaning? Marlowe on the Screen." Sight and Sound, Summer 1973.

Haskell, Molly. Review of Thieves Like Us. Village Voice, February 21, 1974.

_____, and Sarris, Andrew. Reviews of Nashville. Village Voice, June 9, 1975.

Henry, Michael. "Entretien avec Joan Tewkesbury (de John McCabe à Nashville)." Positif 176, December 1975.

_____. "Altmanscope (sur le plateau de Nashville), A Journal of On-Set Observation." Positif 177, January 1976.

_____. "Robert Altman: represres biofilmographiques." Positif 193, September 1977.

Hogue, Peter. Review of The Long Goodbye. Movietone News #25, September 1973.

Jameson, Richard T. "Nashville: Writin' It Down Kinda

Makes Me Feel Better. " Movietone News #43,
September 4, 1975.

_____, and Murphy, Kathleen. "... they take on their
life...." Movietone News #55, September 1977.

Jebb, Julian. Review of Three Women. Sight and Sound,
Autumn 1977.

Jensen, Paul. "The Writer: Raymond Chandler and the
World You Live In. " Film Comment 10, November-
December 1974.

Kael, Pauline. Review of M*A*S*H. New Yorker, January
24, 1970.

_____. Review of Brewster McCloud. New Yorker,
January 9, 1971.

_____. Review of McCabe and Mrs. Miller. New York-
er, July 3, 1971.

_____. Review of Images. New Yorker, December 23,
1972.

_____. Review of The Long Goodbye. New Yorker,
October 22, 1973.

_____. Review of Thieves Like Us. New Yorker, Feb-
ruary 4, 1974.

_____. Review of Nashville. New Yorker, March 3,
1975.

Kinder, Marsha. "The Return of the Outlaw Couple. " Film
Quarterly, Summer 1974.

_____. "The Art of Dreaming in Three Women and
Providence: Structures of the Self. " Film Quarterly,
Fall 1977.

Kolker, Robert Philip. "Night to Day. " Sight and Sound,
Autumn 1974.

Landau, Jon. "Day for Night. " Rolling Stone, December 6,
1973.

_____. Review of Nashville. Rolling Stone, July 31,
    1975.

_____. Review of Thieves Like Us. Rolling Stone,
    April 25, 1974.

McCarthy, Todd. "The Delinquents," in King of the B's.
    McCarthy and Charles Flynn, eds. New York:
    Dutton, 1975.

Macklin, Anthony F. "The Artist and the Multitude Are
    Natural Enemies." Film Heritage 12, 2, Winter
    1976-77.

_____. "Nashville: America's Voices." Film Heritage
    11, 1, Fall 1975.

Meltzer, Richard. Review of Thieves Like Us. Take One
    4, 2, March 1974.

Michener, Charles. An untitled interview with Robert Alt-
    man. Film Comment, September-October 1978.

Milne, Tom. Review of California Split. Sight and Sound,
    Winter 1974-75.

_____. Review of Buffalo Bill and the Indians. Sight
    and Sound, Autumn 1976.

_____. Review of A Wedding. Sight and Sound, Winter
    1978-79.

Monaco, James. "Welcome to Palm Springs (Three Women)
    and Welcome to L. A. (Welcome to L. A.)." Film/
    Literature Quarterly, Spring 1978.

Murphy, Kathleen. "The Long Goodbye: Blues for Mr.
    Chandler." Movietone News #29, January 2, 1974.

Nolan, Jack Edmund. "Notes sur les films TV de Robert
    Altman." Positif 197, September 1977.

Oliver, Bill. "The Long Goodbye and Chinatown: Debunk-
    ing the Private Eye Tradition." Literature/Film
    Quarterly, Summer 1975.

Pittman, Bruce. "Tracking Altman's Movies [on his sound

techniques]. " Take One 5, 3, August 1976.

Robinson, David.   Review of The James Dean Story.   Sight
    and Sound, August 1957.

Rosenbaum, Jonathan.   "Improvisations and Interactions in
    Altmanville. "  Sight and Sound, Spring 1975.

_____.  Rosenbaum, Jonathan.  "An Altman. "  Film
    Comment, September-October 1978.

Rosenthal, Stuart.   "Robert Altman. "  International Film
    Guide.   Peter Cowie, ed.   London:   Tantivity Press,
    1975.

Rubenstein, Roberta.   Review of Brewster McCloud.   Film
    Quarterly, Winter 1971-72.

Sarris, Andrew.   Review of M*A*S*H.   Village Voice, Jan-
    uary 29, 1970.

_____.  Review of Brewster McCloud.   Village Voice,
    December 24, 1970.

_____.  Review of McCabe and Mrs. Miller.   Village
    Voice, July 8, 1971.

_____.  Review of Images.   Village Voice, March 15,
    1973.

_____.  Review of The Long Goodbye.   Village Voice,
    November 8, 1973.

_____.  Review of Buffalo Bill and the Indians.   Village
    Voice, July 4, 1976.

_____.  "Altman at Armageddon. "  Village Voice, Feb-
    ruary 19, 1979.

Self, Robert.   "Invention and Death:   The Commodities of
    Media in Robert Altman's Nashville. "  Journal of
    Popular Film, 5, 3 and 4, 1976.

Sherman, Bill.   Review of Nashville.   Take One 5, 1,
    February 1976.

Siegel, Joal.   "Gnashville. "  Film Heritage 11, 1, Fall 1975.

Stabiner, Karen.   Review of Buffalo Bill and the Indians.
    Film Quarterly,  Fall 1976.

Stewart, Garrett.   "The Long Goodbye from Chinatown. "
    Film Quarterly,  Winter 1974-75.

Stone, Elizabeth.   Review of A Wedding.   Viva,  October
    1978.

Tarrantino, Michael.   "Movement as Metaphor:  The Long
    Goodbye. "   Sight and Sound,  Spring 1975.

Tavernier, Bertrand.   "D. W. Griffith se porte bien, moi
    aussi, merci!"   Positif 120,  October 1970.

Tewkesbury, Joan.   "Dialogue on Film. "   American Film,
    March 1979.

Williams, Alan.   Review of California Split.   Film Quarter-
    ly,  Spring 1975.

Wood, Robin.   "Smart-ass & Cutie-pie:  Notes Towards an
    Evaluation of Altman. "   Movie 21,  Autumn 1975.

# INDEX

for are all but eliminated.   In this sense (although its
themes are reversed), M*A*S*H is very much like Brewster
McCloud, which is flawed by its protagonist's highly unten-
able assumption of control.   In M*A*S*H, there is never
really any doubt who the heroes are, or whether or not they
will succeed.   This in turn leads to characterizations that
sacrifice important subtleties of personality to a more conventional type of spectator identification.

The "dreamers" in M*A*S*H are the "regular army
clowns."   Because of their inability to adjust to the exigen-
cies of this topsy-turvy situation, their chances of surviving
are very slim.   They insist on playing everything by the book,
oblivious to the fact that sanity in this case demands that the
book be totally rewritten.   Consequently, they become out-
casts who, cut off from their own community, must either
readjust or go over the edge.   Major Frank Burns (Robert
Duvall) is M*A*S*H's foremost "dreamer."   By every avail-
able criterion, he simply does not fit in.   This is apparent
from the first time that we see Burns, teaching Ho-Jon (the
Korean "houseboy") how to read the Bible.   In direct contrast, Duke suggests that he read a "picture" (girlie) book.
Burns doesn't drink.   Duke and Hawkeye teach Ho-Jon how
to tend bar.   When Burns reads his Bible while his fellow
tent-mates are trying to enjoy their drinks, Duke asks him,
"Were you on this religious kick at home or did you crack
up here?"   As if to confirm this observation, the camera
now moves from an extreme close-up of Burns to a group
of passersby who are singing a mocking chorus of "Onward,
Christian Soldiers."   These none-too-subtle innuendoes are
followed by a more direct form of action during the very
next scene, as Duke and Hawkeye ask the colonel to get
Burns out of their tent.

Interspersed with these early actions are three brief
scenes that are calculated to ensure the credibility of our
heroes.   In the first of these scenes, Altman's moving camera familiarizes us with the operating tent in which Hawkeye
is now working.   Amidst overwhelming blood and gore, Hawkeye asks a nurse for a clamp, only to have her scratch his
nose with it.   Next, while Dago Red (Rene Auberjonois) begins to administer extreme unction to a dead soldier, Duke
calls on him for some much-needed assistance, saying, "This
man's alive, that one's dead."   The third scene combines
Hawkeye and Duke's blend of irreverent humor and pragmatic dedication with yet another element of endearment.   This
occurs when a group of onlookers cast an admiring glance

(through a glass wall) on the surgeons, whose muffled dialogue and casual humor are barely audible beneath their surgical masks.

Meanwhile, our third good-guy cum chest-cutter has just arrived in the person of Trapper John (Elliott Gould). When questioned by Hawkeye and Duke, he's suspiciously aloof at first, but quickly proves his mettle by accepting a martini. Then, when he plucks a jar of olives from his coat pocket (to the rapt astonishment of Hawkeye and Duke), we simply know that he's right up there with the other guys. This insight is confirmed shortly thereafter when Trapper John flattens Major Burns. The only problem is that the sentiment is laid on a little too thick, for what motivates Trapper is a strikingly manipulative little scene he has just witnessed, involving Burns and Boone (Bud Cort). It occurs in the operating tent when the major accuses Boone of killing his patient by bringing over the wrong needle. The young man is stunned, unbelieving, and we sympathize with him as he breaks down in tears. Given this slant, Burns surely deserves the worst he can get--except that Burns is a person, too.

Characteristically, Burns's recompense (the first in a series) is delayed by a rather abrupt cut to the newly arrived Major Houlihan (Sally Kellerman) touring another one of the wards. This strategic move is a good example of how Altman consistently attempts to integrate what Robin Wood refers to as "overt devices" with more naturalistic techniques. This is, conventional narrative procedure would call for Trapper to get his licks in without any intervening action (as Duke does in the novel). In general, Altman uses these overt devices (elliptical editing, zooms, focus-pulling, self-referentiality) to assert a highly subjective vision that runs counter to the tenets of illusionism. The zoom in particular has become a famous Altman signature (a way of manifesting his presence) which is both overtly manipulative and often highly ambiguous in terms of its narrative implications. In the present instance, Altman uses editing techniques that call attention to themselves (by breaking up the flow of the narrative) to achieve a similar purpose.

Altman's increasingly self-reflexive use of the P. A. system in M*A*S*H is another overt device closely aligned with his elliptical cutting patterns. Usually used as a link between scenes, we first hear the P. A. just after Hawkeye and Duke have arrived at the camp. In this first instance, however, it is merely an integral part of the action, as it mingles with the other overlapping conversations that take place in the tent. The next time it crops up, Altman cuts directly to the P. A. speaker to achieve a transition between an early operating scene and Hawkeye and Duke's second confrontation with Burns. But although it begins as a rather naturalistic technique, future transmissions become more and more overt in their omnipresent mixture of Radio Tokyo broadcasts and humorous pronouncements. Typical of Altman's (smart-ass?) sense of humor, these quips frequently involve drugs (i. e., the missing amphetamines and the announcement that marijuana has been found to be a dangerous drug), and sex (the P. A. orders "short arm inspection," all pinups and nude photos to be taken down, and later countermands a previous request for urine specimens). Sometimes the P. A. even comments on the action, as is the case with the marijuana transmission that is heard over a truly dangerous operation.

An even more "overt" way in which the P. A. is employed to expose the sutures of illusionism has to do with its numerous filmic references. Beginning innocently enough with an announcement for When Willie Comes Marching Home, these transmissions carry a burgeoning, self-reflexive impact that is experienced at several levels. This is due in part to the fact that the announced films (which also include The Halls of Montezuma and The Glory Brigade, among others) are all real war movies about World War II. However, Altman cannot resist calling their "reality" (and M*A*S*H's) into question by having his unidentified P. A. announcer promote them with actual ad copy (". . . a story so big that only the biggest screens can bring it all to you"). Moreover, because the characters never see or refer to these films in any way, we get the distinct impression that these announcements are meant solely for the audience. Consequently, they make us all the more aware that we're watching a movie by calling attention to the illusionist pretense (of "objective reality") of most Hollywood films, and by replacing them with admittedly subjective, self-reflexive techniques.

Ostensibly this strategy would seem to be designed to break the illusionist trance and encourage the kind of audience response heretofore described as "active" or "resonant." But the question that we must soon confront is whether M*A*S*H actually offers a viable alternative, or merely places us in a modernist (anti-illusionist) trance. Before answering this, however, we would do well to examine several other aspects of M*A*S*H's constructions. Returning

first to the film's conception of its community, there are
still several key members who need to be filled in.   One of
these characters is the Painless Pole (John Schuck), the
company dentist.

Although Painless does not appear in the flesh during
his first extended scene, this little vignette tells us a lot
about his relationship to the M*A*S*H community, for the
men all line up outside his shower, just hoping to get a look
at "the best equipped dentist" in the U. S. Army.   As we
soon find out, Painless also runs an ongoing poker game in
his dental clinic.   Typically, his shower scene ends with a
line of "throwaway" humor (because the unidentified speaker
and his companion are walking out of frame), but there is
no mistaking the community's sense of admiration for the
Pole.

Major ("Hot Lips") Houlihan, on the other hand, has
a great deal more difficulty fitting in.   When we first witness her arrival, Hot Lips inadvertently exhibits her long,
stocking-clad legs while exiting a helicopter.   If nothing
else, her physical attributes would seem to qualify Hot Lips
as a welcome addition to the M*A*S*H community.   But
when she strikes up an immediate friendship with Frank
Burns, we know that something is amiss.   This, too, is
confirmed moments later during the sequence in the operating tent in which the power goes off.   True to form,
everyone carries on with the aid of flashlights and lanterns,
singing "When the Lights Go On Again All Over the World"
while Hawkeye and Hot Lips engage in verbal battle.   Once
again the spontaneous, or "improvised," quality of the song
combined with the overlapping dialogue to reinforce the previously established sense of community which Hot Lips is
obviously not yet ready to join, for, to Hawkeye's chagrin,
she not only insists on defending Burns but is so petty that
she argues that "Hawkeye" is "an inefficient term. "  He
ends the conversation by branding her "a regular army
clown. "

Since they are the only two "dreamers" in the camp,
Hot Lips and Burns feel a natural attraction for each other.
But because they are so predictable, the way in which Altman sets the scene for their first rendezvous is a lot more
intriguing than the actual encounter.   Thus, after Colonel
Blake leaves the camp on army business, everyone else (except Hot Lips and Burns) parties in a darkly lit tent.   Altman then uses the utter darkness outside as a transition